T0161932

Making **MEN** *from* "The Boys"

Making
MEN
"The *from* Boys"

WINNING
LIFE LESSONS
Every Young Man
Needs to Succeed

NICK OLYNYK

New York

Making MEN *from* "The Boys"

WINNING LIFE LESSONS *Every Young Man Needs to Succeed*

© 2015 **NICK OLYNYK**.

Published in New York, New York, by Morgan James Publishing. Morgan James and The Entrepreneurial Publisher are trademarks of Morgan James, LLC.
www.MorganJamesPublishing.com

The Morgan James Speakers Group can bring authors to your live event. For more information or to book an event visit The Morgan James Speakers Group at
www.TheMorganJamesSpeakersGroup.com.

A **free** eBook edition is available
with the purchase of this print book.

CLEARLY PRINT YOUR NAME ABOVE IN UPPER CASE

Instructions to claim your free eBook edition:
1. Download the BitLit app for Android or iOS
2. Write your name in **UPPER CASE** on the line
3. Use the BitLit app to submit a photo
4. Download your eBook to any device

ISBN 978-1-63047-521-5 paperback
ISBN 978-1-63047-522-2 eBook
Library of Congress Control Number:
2014921290

Cover Design by:
Rachel Lopez
www.r2cdesign.com

Interior Design by:
Bonnie Bushman
bonnie@caboodlegraphics.com

In an effort to support local communities and raise awareness and funds, Morgan James Publishing donates a percentage of all book sales for the life of each book to Habitat for Humanity Peninsula and Greater Williamsburg.

Get involved today, visit
www.MorganJamesBuilds.com

Habitat
for Humanity®
Peninsula and
Greater Williamsburg
Building Partner

"It is no use saying, 'We are doing our best';
you have got to succeed in doing what is necessary."
—Sir Winston Churchill

TABLE OF CONTENTS

Preface
WHY I LOVE HOCKEY

I love hockey.

I can't describe my feelings about the sport in a purer way. For anybody who has laced up skates, touched a hardened scar on their face, or received a pat on the ass after potting a goal, you already know what I mean. And for those who are fans, there is nothing like the excitement in the rink, that combination of appreciating fine art on ice combined with the blood and guts of battle. Character is a huge part of the game. The history surrounding hockey, the folklore involved, makes it special. It's the kind of sport you show up for in a suit before playing a game and then go out for a beer after it. Hockey is different.

What I love about the game is what it did for me. It taught me things about myself I didn't yet know. Hockey doesn't lie. You're not a solo athlete—you have to be accountable to your teammates. When you have a sore groin, an ache in your back, or a weakened shoulder, you have to set your own struggles aside and step up and do it for the boys in the room. You're required to reach beyond yourself and act despite your pain and distractions. You must bring emotion to the rink, not hope it comes to you. Hockey forces you to rise up against adversity.

When you battle through that and win, it's a celebration. You're a hero. Your results trail with you. At the face-off dot when that opponent badmouths you, all you have to say is "look at the clock" and the score silences them. While guys mouth off on the ice (and have to answer to it), hockey players are level-headed off of the ice. To the media players say they have to be prepared for the next battle. It's not taunts and shouting into the camera. The guy who rubbed his stinking leather mitt in his opponents face on the ice is a gentleman off of it. He knows how to carry himself.

Perhaps what I love most about the sport is that it really does parallel the real world. You don't see this unless you know the game. The hard work done in private practice creates the winning scores in public games. People recognize winners, and most importantly, you know winning yourself. The results are on the score sheet. Yet, you're also only as good as your last game. Hockey forces you to bring your best every time you step on the ice. You can't duck out early; you can't expect to win on a half-assed effort. This mindset is invaluable in the real world.

Hockey has the ability to make boys into men. If you can't take the physical punishment, you're weeded out at an early age. If you can't face the noise from the coach when you don't perform, you simply won't hit the ice the next game. The winners react and rise up. They take on the challenge and use it to make themselves better players and better men. Those who don't (or can't) won't be part of the club very long.

As a hockey player, if you navigate how the game is played between your ears, you can navigate the game of life as well. Sport is a modern representation of war. In a society with few rites of passage left for young men, hockey is one bastion of strength-forging left. As you play the game, you learn. And as you play the game more and more, it carves you into a man. These are the lessons it teaches you.

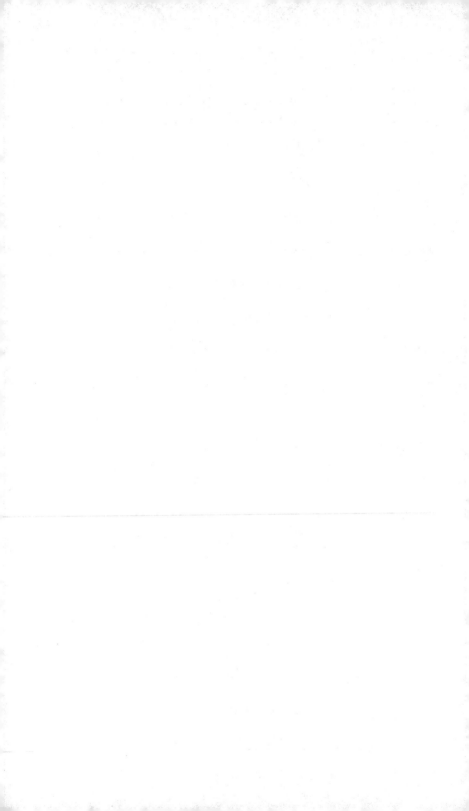

Chapter 1
WINNERS PLAY TO WIN

The coldest place ice can bite you is on that baby-soft patch right under your chin. That bite starts like a tickle and finishes like an upper cut if your chin is near the ice long enough. The dry, frozen air burns on it and enters those softest pores of throat skin like a corrosive gas. When you're lying facedown this part of your throat never actually makes contact with the ground, the ice. It only kisses your chin. Your chin is tough. It will melt that bite away into a soothing, cool little divot if you lay there long enough. But that soft spot between your Adam's apple and chin, that will always get burned by the cold if you don't protect it.

I knew this feeling in an instant. I felt that undeniable burn below my chin right after I felt one on the back of my neck. That frigid bite was from the ice, just as I describe. The burn on the back of my neck was metaphorical—that was the goal light shining on me. We were in Saskatoon and it was my first game of Midget AAA. I was face down staring at the goal post, the puck beside me across the goal line. We were losing.

In Saskatchewan, where I was born, AAA is a pretty big deal. Mothers kiss their sons goodbye at fifteen so they can go play it. Towns rally around their team as if the boys were playing junior. In fact, there were only twelve AAA teams in the province, as many as in junior A. It was elite, and I wasn't fitting in very well so far.

I had no clue what it meant to be a winner. I could respect a player who had won a championship or a team who made the playoffs, but I didn't know the internal aspect of winning. Not yet. Those lessons would start later that season, and they would carry over to the next four years of junior hockey. In this moment, I was just lying on the ice, facedown, staring at the goal post for that eternal second, with the cold air burning my never-shaved neck.

"Christ, Olie, stop something," our d-man said. I should have taken his advice.

Over the course of that period I let in three goals and got pulled. I couldn't complete my first game. We lost. Worse for me, my then-junior team, the Portland Winterhawks, were in the stands watching. The same scout who recommended me to the organization had come to see how his bet had paid off. I met him in the hallway after the game.

I only leaned against the wall for a second as the frost bit my hand and soaked the cuff of my jacket. The rink was pure cement, a large prairie freezer. I put my hands in my pockets and looked him in the eye.

"We want to see you keep developing and we want more out of you. You're in a good spot right now, so we want to keep you here for a while," the scout said.

I didn't want to hear that I would stay the uncertain "while." I wanted news of getting called up to the next level. I wanted to hear that I was in their plans for the future. I wanted the good news I was used to hearing up until then.

I'd played on good teams and bad teams up to that point in my career, if you can call it that at sixteen. On the good ones, I'd be an impact player. I received praise. On the bad ones, the losses weren't my fault. I was the goalie. I should have been bailed out. The old, "We gotta help out our tendy, guys."

Nobody was bailing me out now.

"I just feel there is such an emphasis on winning up here. I thought this was a development league. I thought the goal was to get us ready for the next level. Why do they just talk about wins?"

Naïve stupidity. Pure naïve stupidity. The scout patted me once on the shoulder.

"That's how it is up here, and it's only going to get more demanding. You can't accept losses anymore. The pressure only gets greater from here."

I clenched my teeth and nodded my head. Mission accepted. I had a lot of learning to do if I was going to scratch and claw my way to the next level, rub elbows with future NHL all-stars and battle my way to the top. The clichés rattled around my brain constantly. Over the next few years they would be something that couldn't be glossed over. If I was going to have success I would have to earn it. It wouldn't be handed to me, and I wouldn't get second chances when I screwed up.

And every time I did screw up, I would earn a lesson about what *not* to do. Do what you're not supposed to do enough times and you'll have enough lessons to write a book about winning. In that hallway, I had just received lesson number one.

Redefining Winning

The number one culprit lynching men of their success today is a weak mindset. This book is written for young men who are striving for more success in life. (Of course, it will work for any young hockey player too.) The lessons are learned from my years of playing hockey at all levels, including the highest of junior. It has been nine years since I last played junior hockey and the lessons have impacted me greatly now as an adult. The impact hockey has had on my life is undeniable. If you've played the game with your heart and soul, you'll know what I mean.

Since my days of hockey I've become a coach in many areas, but not a traditional hockey coach. I've started a company, the Junior Hockey Truth. At JHT, I create products and provide advice for bantam and midget hockey players and their parents about how to succeed at junior hockey. It is my way of giving back to a sport that gave me so much.

Over my years in hockey, I've noticed that elite players are unique individuals. They strive to improve. You give these guys a task and they make no excuses. They push back against the world when the world seems to turn against them… And they steer their lives in the right direction with that push. However, it's not this way for everybody. Not every young man has figured out winning yet. I see too many young men who only play the game of life not to lose, and I see this sentiment growing. Too many young men are content to play it safe. They're happy just to tie.

So what created this culture of playing not to lose? I would blame the creators of phrases like these:

"You win as long as you try."

"Make friends and have fun."

"Fun is the name of the game."

These platitudes sound like something an over-protective mother would say to her pouty five year-old.

Fun is not the name of the game. Winning is why you play the game. Hockey is just a pure form and physical manifestation of real-world battles. When a man loses his job and has a mortgage payment due, does he go into the next job interview saying, "As long as I try, that's all I can ask for?" Or does he go in there with conviction and a burning desire to show what he can offer the company? The world rewards those who put something back into it. People who *produce* results get rewarded. They win.

Today's generation of men lack one key thing that generations of the past had—a war, a Great Depression, a gold rush. Now I'm not saying that war is a good thing. But what I am saying is that generations of the past had a defining moment. Their men had a rite of passage, a battle to toughen them. Today's boys have their battles fought by an overprotective school system and politically correct society. These constructions commend giving participation ribbons over learning to deal with winning and losing. Where is the chance for growth through adversity and accomplishment when a young man doesn't get a chance to make his own stand and prove himself?

Fortunately, if you're a reader of this book, you probably were or are a hockey player, or you are close to one, or simply love the game itself. If so, you'll likely have an idea of the importance of winning. You likely have at least one foot in the success lane already and know that you have capabilities. Throughout this book, you'll be forced to re-examine your initial success in life and also what keeps you from full achievement. Every example provided is tied to the game of hockey so you'll understand where I'm coming from.

From this point on, vow that you will not accept anything less than wins. Ties are not good enough. To get to the top of the pack, you only accept W's from now on. Sound good? With that, let's begin building your winner's mindset.

Exercises – How they work

You'll see throughout this book that each chapter starts off with a real hockey story from my playing days, followed by a lesson. (Most but not all names of former teammates and coaches, some NHLers, have been changed.) After each lesson is an exercise you can do to improve your winner's mindset. Some of these lessons take some deep thought and introspection. Most you won't complete in the minute it takes to read them. Feel free to let them ruminate in your head. Keep a note in your phone where you can write down ideas you have about them throughout the day. But most importantly, make sure you do them! Anything I advise in here I have lived through myself, so I know how difficult it can be to enter self-examination. Play through the pain if that's what it takes to get the result. You'll be thankful for it in the long run.

Chapter 2
WINNERS HAVE PURPOSE

Another loss meant another 3 a.m. lecture. We'd unload our gear, exhausted from a four-hour post-game bus ride. Then we'd sit. And sit. And sit. We'd all sit in a two lines of folding chairs in "the dungeon" waiting for Lloyd to yell at us.

He walked into the room, hands in his pockets, gazing at the floor. You could hear our lounge's blue lights buzz.

"I want to teach you guys a lesson." He paused. "All night you guys were lost out there."

He paused again and thought.

"When you've got a nose like mine, you know what your role is," he said, pulling a hand out of his pocket and pointing at his face. "We need sacrifice out there…You've never had a doctor stick forceps up your nose after an elbow to the face, have you Davey?" He stepped right up to Kyle Davis and towered over him in his chair. Kyle shook his head.

"I didn't think so. It's because you're soft. We lose games because you play soft. You bitch because the lounge ping-pong table is broken and you don't have a TV in the dressing room. But guess what? You don't deserve a TV. Winners get a TV. Winners get a ping-pong table. This place is not the fuckin' country club anymore, Davey."

I had seen this charade before. Lloyd would get right up in somebody's face, usually a guy already in a bad slump, and then he'd dig into him. He'd looked you straight in the eyes, and you'd try not to stare back at the only clean scar on his face. The scar cut down the middle of his nose. It was clean because that is where the surgeon had to slice him open to rebuild that hook on his face after he broke it for the tenth time. The other scars were dirty and jagged, like leather torn on a barbwire fence. They came from sticks slashing his chin and knuckles landing on his cheekbones.

The truth was that every time he got right up in your face, his intermission coffee breath reeking inside your nose, you were forced to learn something from those rotten words he spit at you.

"Now you listen and you listen good: I do not care whether you love me or you hate me. I'm not here to make friends. But I'm going to make a winner out of you." He stood straight and looked down the line. "I'm going to make winners out of all of you. I'll do whatever it takes, and you can thank me later, so help me God."

Often times, we did hate him. I was told early on by a veteran not to expect praise. If the coach wasn't yelling at you that meant you were doing well. We got yelled at…a lot. Then he'd soften up and try to impart a lesson, albeit by singling somebody out.

"Murray, why are you here?" he said, staring down at a shaggy head of blond hair.

"I'm here to play hockey."

Lloyd walked down, slowly, to meet Murray face to face.

"No. Why are you here? Why did we bring you here? Tell me why you aren't on the oil rigs right now in minus forty with your beer-drinking buddies? Huh? What is your purpose on this club?"

Murray took a second and looked at the floor. A couple of the boys lifted their heads out of their hands. Somebody rattled an ice bag.

"I'm a digger. My job is to plant my ass in front of the net in their end and to get greasy along the boards in our end. I get the puck out, I go hard in the corners and I back-check through the middle. That's my job."

I liked Murray. He was one of those players that lived for the boys, a "beauty," as they are called. These were the guys who knew they were either going to slug it out in the minors, or head back to their family farm or the oil rigs or a pulp mill. Some dead end. They played because they loved the game, yet they always had to eat shit from the coach.

Even though Lloyd said he didn't care if we loved him or hated him, he loved these guys the most, the diggers earning scars. That's why he yelled at them the most. They had the toughest role. They weren't put on the ice to score. They scored with their face and their fists. The only thing separating them from the coach was thirty years of age and eight broken noses. As much of an asshole as Lloyd could be, he nurtured these guys. Yelling was nurturing in the dressing room. Lloyd was once one of these guys. He still wanted to be one of these guys. You could see his disgust to lose this much. That's why you indulged him during these two hour, 3 a.m. tirades. We knew there was something to learn when he spoke.

"You're damn right, Murray. That is your job. Now everybody knows your job." Lloyd turned back to look down the line at the rest of us. "When you know what your purpose is, crystal clear, only then can you do your job properly. If we're going to turn this ship around, each and every one of you needs to know your purpose on this club. Only then can we become winners. And you don't need a nose like mine to become one."

Finding Your Purpose

As a player moves up the ranks in hockey, he doesn't just fall into a role: he embraces one. That role is what makes him important, and a successful player chooses to fill it like nobody else could. This role gives him confidence and a sense of entitlement to fill it. If he fills this role—his purpose—well enough he can make it into a successful career.

A problem I see with many young men is that they lack purpose. They don't know why they do the things they do. You can ask them, "Why do you do your job? What do you want to achieve before you retire? What keeps you doing what you do?"

The standard answers fall into the trap of, "I needed a job after college," "The pay is good," or "This is just temporary until I find something else."

These aren't winning answers.

Every winner needs a vision—a life's mission—that drives him to shoot straight up out of bed each morning. If you're trading your valuable, valuable time for a career, business, or job that doesn't serve your greater mission in life, you're wasting your life as a man. You're the grinder not going into the corners, the scorer not driving to the net.

On every hockey team, different players serve different roles. Ask any fighter playing three minutes per game if he is important to the team, and he'll puff up his chest and answer "yes." Does he score goals? Maybe not, but he understands when that one shift comes each period he needs make use of it. He knows what he is put on the ice to do and why he is on the team. He may be called a fighter, but his purpose isn't just to fight. It's to protect teammates, keep order and give a spark when needed. He has impact. This guy will do more bag skates and train harder in the summer than almost any other player because he knows that is what it takes to maintain his scarce role. There is no question—he understands his purpose.

If your main purpose is going to a job where you can't wait to get home and play video games, you are not living your purpose. All the money earned from work won't bring you core fulfillment when it drains you of your masculinity. You must go deeper. You need something greater to build toward.

The core step to finding your purpose is to ask, "Why?" Why do you go to work each day? Why did you decide to get a university degree? Why do you want more money?

For the longest time, I didn't know my "whys." Like many major junior hockey graduates, I ended up getting a university degree because it was free. I was always told to go to school, use hockey as a means to an end. Get a degree because that is the minimum to get a good job. I just accepted this as fate. Make the NHL or get a degree. A degree wasn't the worst thing in the world to get, but I didn't know why I personally wanted it. In many ways I didn't want it. I just thought it was what you do. Get a degree, get a job, get a white picket fence and marry the first girl. I asked myself, "Who says this way should be 'the way' for me? Why?"

By my third year of university, I'd given up hope of ever using a degree. I had found an answer for my "why." I found a purpose.

The truth is that I didn't want a job—I wanted what I thought a good job represented—money that led to freedom. (I believe the number one thing all men want is more freedom and choice in how they live their lives.) That freedom would let me impact the world. If I had freedom I could be around hockey forever and help other hockey players. My intrinsic drive up to that point was not to be poor and not to look bad to friends and family. However, once I found my why—money that leads to freedom so I can help hockey players—everything shifted. I realized that if what I truly wanted was freedom, there were much better ways to get it than a respectable but boring job. I couldn't play in the NHL, but hockey could still be my life. I just needed the freedom to pursue it.

Immediately, I shifted all of my classes for the next semester to be on a single day. Once per week I'd endure an 8 a.m. to 8 p.m. marathon sitting in desks that were way too small for me. The other six days were mine. Being in the arts program I realized that if I put my face in front of the professor and merely handed in the essays, it would be impossible to fail. 'D' for degree.

In those six other days each week, I started chasing greater pursuits. I took the spare time to learn how to write sales copy. This was what I wanted to learn in school but was never taught. In time, I moved from sales copy to writing e-books. If you've never written anything before, it can be a real test to do it every single day. Knowing my whys got my hands on the keyboard. While other guys played video games, I worked. Eventually, my sales writing got me an internship offer with a coaching company that trained me in real-world skills. Occasionally, I would fly to their seminars around North America. By my fourth year of university, I'd be at a marketing meet-up in Manhattan while my classmates were at a kegger near campus. My purpose was no longer essays and classes, at least in my mind. Eventually, I ran out of money to go on these trips, but I didn't want to let this deter me. I couldn't let a lack of funds eat my purpose. Ultimately, I took a job flipping burgers. (That's the best I could get while in university.) It wasn't exactly a win, but I knew it afforded me more time to travel and thus more learning opportunities. Knowing why I was flipping those burgers made it endurable. It forwarded my purpose.

I finished my BA and already had some smart contracts and contacts established. (Being an ex-major junior hockey player, I had no student loans either.) I had started on my own path. Flipping burgers isn't exactly exciting and arguing with professors about missing classes to travel didn't do me a lot of favors. However, there was no question in my mind: I had to grind it out. It just became self-evident to do these things once I knew my whys. I was like the fighter who learned to swing and jab my way onto a team—this was my training camp of life.

If you understand why you do the things you do, you too will know your purpose. The tough times will become something you grind through and the good times will become one of many signposts on your journey. It's not always easy to find your purpose, but when you do, providence shifts. New opportunities appear where you were blind to them before. You have vigor to get up each day. You gain masculinity and power as a man.

You may not be exactly where you want to be just yet, but the belief that you'll get there pulls you toward what you demand from life and yourself. The strength in that belief comes from your whys.

Exercise

To find your whys:

1. Write down three components of your life. These can be things that make up your identity (career, goals) or things that you do (going to the gym, playing video games). These should make up your purpose. If they don't, note that.
2. Ask yourself what you ultimately want to achieve in life and what you want out of it (Be a father who has time for his kids, retire early, buy a cottage at the lake, own a hockey team.)
3. For each of your components in number one, ask yourself why you do them. Dig deep. For example, going to work because you want money is not an answer. What does the money get you? An easy way to find your whys is to answer these questions:
    *   Why do I do X?
    *   What keeps me doing X?
    *   When did I first know that I wanted to do X?

- What will X ultimately get me?
- How does it feel to do X?

4. Compare your answer for number two to your answers in number three. Does what you do align with what you want to achieve?

5. Make a list of three things you can do immediately to start pulling you toward what you want in number two. Once you take the first step, within a week make a plan to implement step two.

Chapter 3
WINNERS HAVE SYSTEMS

I was a professional spectator in major junior hockey. I did a lot more watching than playing for those two defining seasons. I watched the boys throw their hands up after a win and drop their heads after a loss. It was part of my role. As a backup goalie, I watched the 5000 fans, who in turn watched me sitting, and I had the best seat in the house—right on the bench. That's being a backup.

There are two kinds of backup goalies at any level. The first kind are young; the up and coming rookies. These guys are talented but still figuring out how to approach the game at a higher level. The coach will also cut them some slack. I started as this type. However, in my second year of junior, I was past that stage—I was the second kind of pine rider, the dependable veteran. The dependable veteran may have been a starter previously, or he is always adequate at filling in when the starter needed a rest, but he'll never be a superstar. I should have epitomized this role as the backup to Carey Price. However, in that dependable veteran role, I wasn't all that dependable. I didn't have a winning system and it bit me the hardest on the road.

Carey and I would room together on the road. When I would get up on game day he was still sleeping. He probably needed it. For every ten games he played, I'd get one. On the night of this story, we would play the Kelowna Rockets, the defending national champions. I came out of the shower perked up and refreshed.

"Are you starting tonight?" I asked him.

"I thought you were."

"Don didn't tell me anything, so it's your turn."

Usually, the coach would let you know if you were starting a few days in advance of a road trip. Sometimes it was the day before a game. Not this day though. I hated being in the lurch of not knowing when I'd play. Yet when you're the backup, you have to be cool and ready—always ready—without an actual reason to be prepared. It's the oddest job on the team.

And as a backup to the world's best junior goalie, you go so long between games that every start feels like the first exhibition game after summer. The familiar shouts from the stands of "sieve" and "Olynyk sucks" rise above the cheers. The puck shots echo off the boards like cannon blasts. The game moves at warp speed. You're the born-again virgin every time you play. You can't remember the last time you slide in the net, and that makes it tough to put in a solid performance—let alone see how long you can last in there.

Carey dressed and we headed down to breakfast. The same buffet spread, standard in every hotel—eggs poured from a carton, gristly crisp bacon and a pre-buttered pile of toast. The coaches were already eating. I wished the assistant would come over and tell me when I was playing. You never knew when that signal would be given, and it was important.

Winners have a certain way of preparing for success. They have systems. When they focus on their systems, the systems do the work. As a backup, I didn't have a solid system. I had two half-assed ones—one for when I was starting and one for when I was on the bench. On the day of this game, I didn't know which one to use. The amount of breakfast I ate would be proportional to me starting or not. If I didn't start, I'd want a light breakfast because I'd have a long morning skate ahead of me. If I did start, I'd probably load up on toast to drive as much carbs into my system as possible in the morning. That way I could eat a lighter pre-game meal. The preparation to win starts early.

The coaches rose up from their corner table. The assistant coach walked through our section.

"Bus will leave at nine-fifteen. Skate at ten," he said. No sign of who was starting. I was silent on the ride to the rink, wondering how to prepare.

We walked in the back door of Kelowna's Prospera Place. I loathed the uncertain feeling as I stopped and stared at the ice. During a morning skate, the arena is an empty vessel. It's not the same arena you play in at night. The floodlights still shine bright but their deep buzz is loud. They shine on all of those empty seats and that buzz forces you to realize there will be screaming fans in them that evening. That buzz calls you to be ready. It teases you and haunts you if you're unprepared.

With most morning skates, you don't have time to prepare. You simply slap on your pads and hit the ice. I swore that half the time they were just an excuse to get us out of bed. Few players liked practice this early.

"Do you have to put your fuckin' pads right in my way, Olie?" said Cam, sitting next to me. "You're the backup. We should put you in the hall."

As I geared up, Don walked in with a folded sheet of paper in one hand and a marker in the other. The room quieted down in anticipation of the lineup. On the wall was a board with a rink outline on it, the kind for drawing plays between periods. He wrote out the roster. First, the forwards lines, starting with the first down to the fourth; then the d-pairings, starting with the top pair down to the third. Then he wrote "Price—Olynyk" on an equal line.

Carey had a wide spot to himself across the room, the kind seemingly built for the starting goalie. Don stared across the room at me and glanced at Carey. Then he exited. No indication of the starting goalie.

Cam nudged me. "Now whose head do I know to shoot at?" He had such a greasy smile, that shit-eating grin.

The backup serves a different purpose in the morning skate. These mini-practices can be as simple as three warm-up drills or as intense as a full-blown practice. It all depends where you are in the lineup. The top guys are done after fifteen minutes. They get loose and get off. The bottom feeders like me could be out for another hour of what's called conditioning. As the backup, I was well-conditioned to skate lengths of the ice until I felt like puking. You are the most drilled player who never plays. But when you are playing, when you're the starter, oh man, it's nice. You take those easy warm-up shots off the wall, steer the rebounds to the corner and feel like a champion. When you're the man for your team, you almost feel like you're the one warming them up. You're doing them a favor by being out there. You exit proud and early. Of course, in reality, the forwards keep the shots down for you and shoot off the wall. They aim for your gloves, not the top corner. They pick a target to hit, and you're that target. You want that as a starter.

When you're the backup, the target is your head. The forwards skate the length of the ice, cut in at the top of the circles and rip one at the roof. They cheer when they score. You're out there to challenge them so when they beat you it builds their confidence. Confidence is built at both ends of the rink. At one end for the starter, at the other for the rest of the guys via the backup.

We took to the ice and skated the customary warm-up laps.

"You starting today, Olie?" said Grease, a rookie who was dicking around in the hall when the lineup was put up. I didn't know if he wanted to shoot at my head or if I was paranoid.

"Don't know yet."

The coach blew his whistle, and without his having to say anything the forwards all went to separate corners to do a horseshoe warm-up. In my net, I jabbed my gloves together and glided out past the blue paint of the crease.

Get your stick on everything low, track the puck in, put 'em in the corner, I thought to myself as Grease came flying down the wall. He released a quick wrister. *TINK*, the first shot went right off my head. It was almost too predictable. One corner cheered. "Keep 'em down!" somebody yelled from another. "He might start today."

Over the next fifteen minutes I received a mix of shots, some in the top corners, some straight at my pads. Nobody knew where to shoot. I couldn't build a rhythm. My system for preparing to start was out of whack. I needed that system. When my system was in place, my brain locked in. I would get in the zone, as they say. But today, I was the backup starter. System failure due to lack of configuration.

After twenty minutes of drills, Don blew his whistle one last time. The vets got off the ice. The rookies waited to pick up pucks. The scratches waited to skate after the rookies left. Don skated over to me.

"How'd you feel today, Olie?" he said. When a coach wants honesty, he's nice.

"Pretty good."

"Think you can play tonight?"

I felt I could go every night. How I felt I would perform was a different thing at this point in my career. Don always wanted conviction in an answer.

"I think so."

"What the fuck does 'I think so' mean? I'm asking you if you're ready to fucking win tonight. Or do you want me to play him?" He waved his stick toward the other end of the rink.

"I'll be ready coach, to win," I said, looking him straight in the eye.

"Good. We're going to need you. This is your chance to show these guys what you've got. I know you can."

He slapped me on the pads with his stick, the swipe of confidence, and skated away.

This was rare. For one, the coach was nearly friendly with me, with words of encouragement nevertheless. Coaches were usually only friendly with the veterans, and even then it was friendly but businesslike. And second, a coach never waited to watch the pre-game skate to see who to start. Usually my starts were planned weeks in advance. The schedule dictated it. That was part of the system we all followed. The staff looked at when Carey would need a rest, and then they'd try to find a game for me that wasn't crucial or that we were very much expected to lose. In this case, Kelowna was so far ahead of us in the standings that we weren't battling with them for position. The odds were that they'd beat us on home ice too, even if Carey did play. If the coaches were going to give Carey a rest, it would be during a game that we probably couldn't win anyway. Of course, nobody could say that and I couldn't think that. When the odds are against you, you have to look at the situation as a challenge where you can prove yourself. If I could pull out the impossible win from a probable loss, maybe I'd get another start that month.

That night I did my full pre-game routine, my system for starting. I ran, then stretched (for seven minutes, hip to toe), endured the pre-game meeting geared toward everybody but the goalie, stretched again with the team, and got dressed (left skate, right skate; left pad, right pad.) The warm-up was high tempo. The sweat ran off my cheeks and over my lips. I felt good. I felt ready for war.

The dressing room is like a rally hall before a game. There is chatter, then the coach gives his speech, which is paced and long and drawn. Then there is a bit of silence, just long enough that you can hear the lights buzz. A trainer will pop his head in and say "five" and that means you only have a few minutes left before you hit the ice, in the dark, weapons in hand. You can hear the howls and boos float into the air as you step on to the ice, ready to riot. The lights are out and the seats are full. The only cheers are when the home team enters the ice and after that, the anthems.

I hated all the shenanigans before a game—the big announcement of the starting lineup, singing not only the Canadian but also the American anthem, and a ceremonial puck drop. I wanted to step out and play. The more I waited, the more my mind would wander at that stage. The stimuli would grow. You're standing in the blue paint in front of thousands of people who want nothing more than to see you fail. You can think you're ready, but that can unravel. Fast.

Even when you're a nervous goalie, you know you're still able to perform. Your fear is that you'll let *yourself* down. You know you can win, you know you're prepared to play, and you know you can show up to fight within your crease. It's an inward focus. When that puck drops, all you worry about is your game, and when you're on your game, everybody else's game molds around yours. When you're scared, however, you fear that you'll let *teammates* down. This is because you don't trust yourself. You *try* to do your best and you *hope* the chips fall in your favor. You *wish* the game to go your way. When you're not mentally ready for a challenge, you worry about what others think, not about your own game. That's when they light you up.

In less than two minutes, Kelowna popped one past me. Two minutes later, they scored another. Shea Weber put another past me before the ten-minute mark. We were down five to one after the first period, and I was going nowhere. I had to endure this loss. It was Carey's night off. That's why I played once per month. That's why the team played differently. That's why we, the Tri-City Americans, had no chance on paper. My game, my team, my fault.

No shots rang off my head that night, but I wished they did. In fact, I couldn't look anybody in the eye after the game. Not Don, not Cam, not Grease. Half of me was mad because the team was absolutely lifeless. I expected that. Everybody wanted to win, but we were not winners that year. We *tried* to win, but we felt doomed. Carey was a winner and he created this feeling that we could win every night. I was the backup. I blew my one start. I had a whole month to prepare and hone my system and I wasn't ready. I was relying on a ton of external factors to fall into place—the perfect meal, the perfect pre-game skate, the perfect spot in the room—none of which came to me. Winners make their own destiny and winners are prepared to win. They don't win every time, but they believe in their winning system. That system prepares them to win. They force their environment to mold to them. At this point in my career, I wasn't a winner. I was still losing. I didn't see myself as a winner. I had more to learn.

Preparing to Win

There is an old saying that "perfect preparation prevents poor performance." Winners are prepared to win through systems, and the world rewards those who play them properly.

A system is a step-by-step success mechanism that enables you to consistently win over and over. It's a process or series of steps that more often than not will lead to a predictable outcome. If you invest in your process and play it 100 percent, you should be in the best position possible to get your desired result, your win. You can't always control outcomes, but you can control the action you take. That action is the steps within your system. Follow the steps and you win. If you have the right steps, this system-first approach can overcome what is out of your control in the long run.

At the end of a hockey game, the best player on the ice isn't always on the winning team. He can be a very skilled player, but if his team doesn't win he isn't a winner. That's why scouts are always looking for players who've been on winning teams. There is an assumption that winners already know how to win. They're the kind of guys who will find a way to win despite the odds. It doesn't have to be taught to these guys. They know what it takes.

Yet in today's world, there is a real numbness to losing. Starting at a young age, many boys are told to go into sports to "make friends and have fun" because "you only lose if you don't try." Crap.

Sports were invented by the civilized warrior societies of the Greeks and Romans. They were an artificial war spectacle made for entertainment, to chastise criminals (society's losers) and celebrate warriors. Sport can be used to make a young man into warrior. Today, many *grown* men aren't warriors. They haven't gone through the rite of passage that every man needs: a war.

The way to win in a war is to have a plan for each battle that leads to an overall victory. In life, a man needs these battle plans too. So often men have the desire to win and they think that willpower can pull them through. Willpower is not enough.

In this chapter's story, I felt that I had the desire to play and the desire to win. However, at the highest levels of life, desire alone is not enough. A lot of people want and desire a lot of things in this world. Wishing and hoping is not enough. Belief is not enough. These are just the prerequisites to building momentum. With momentum, you can carry through your systems.

For example, in writing this book, I have a system for success I use. Each day I write a minimum of 750 words, six days per week, for a maximum of one hour each day. In doing this, I'll have finished writing the book in four months. I've used this system for three other books I've written and ghostwritten. There are days when I can write 1200 words before I max out on time, and there are days when I struggle to get my 750 down, if at all (which is when the 1200-word days make up for it.) However, I make damn sure that first thing every writing day I sit down and jam out an hour on the keyboard. If I can't type anything, I am forced to sit in my chair for an hour. If I max out on time, I finish my thought and cut it off until the next day. This prevents burnout and also promotes adherence to my system.

My belief and desire to write this book comes and goes. Some days I wonder if my stories will come off as trying too hard, overdramatic or just a washed-up player's diatribe. Other days I feel that I'm spitting gems at the screen as I say the sentences out loud. Regardless, I keep my ass in the chair and I write. This system does the work for me. As one of my coaches once said, "Play the system and let the system do the work."

Every man who wants to be a winner needs to find a winning system and play it. The first place to start is to find somebody who is already winning. Break down what their system for success is. When I was a rookie behind now-NHL goalie Josh Harding for the Regina Pats, I needed to learn rebound control. I watched how he'd shift his hips to angle his pads instead of kicking out his legs. The common cliché of "kicking out" rebounds is false, I learned. After controlling the shot, I'd immediately square up to the puck—get off my knees and realign myself to the rebound—just like I saw Harding do. It became automatic that I would not only control the rebound, but also that I'd be square to a second shot. Regardless of if the initial shot was stationary or on a rush, every practice I squared up so it became automatic in a game. Stand up to the rebounds, sit my ass in the chair and type. The systems do the work.

Once you figure out a success system you have to adapt it to become your own. With my rebounds, I learned how to control them from Josh Harding, but I still wasn't consistent in controlling them. Some days I could cradle them like the Virgin Mary rocked Jesus. Other days they were bouncing back past the shooter. On my next team, Tri-City, I picked up another piece of my system by watching Carey Price. I saw that there was an art to what's called moving into the shot. That meant that when a shot would come at the right corner of the net, I'd shift an inch to the right and meet it. That way, I'd not only be shifting my hips to control it, but I'd also have momentum to get off my knees and square up to the shot. I started doing this in practice. After a year of doing this, plus a few other things, I became an all-star for my team. I took my initial copied system and added new elements.

The best way to add your own elements to a system is through trial and error. A winner can't be afraid to fail. You can only learn to win once you learn to lose. Experiment with your system and try different methods until you find what works. Then you'll have a system to trust.

You also want a system that has you controlling the controllables, not relying on outside factors to fall into place. This is where most guys slip up. If you ever catch yourself saying, "It wasn't my fault" after failing, ask yourself what you could have done differently. Start at the point of failure and work your way back through the events leading up to the loss. This will not only have you taking responsibility for what you can control, but it will also help you find weak points in your system that can be strengthened. If you have a system that works and that you believe in, you will be playing that game against yourself, not external factors. The goal will be for you to play your game. You won't be listening to the crowd or the doubters around you. You'll only worry about playing the system and letting it do the work. As you strengthen your system, you'll figure out what works, and thus believe in your system—yourself— more. It's circular.

If you have a goal you want to achieve—whether that is to be in top form for a hockey game, get in shape or grind out the extra time needed for a project at work—you're going to want to put a winner's system in place.

Exercise

Here are the steps to creating a winner's system:

1. Identify the desired outcome. Before you create a system, you have to know what you specifically want to achieve. Make sure it is traceable. If you had a six-pack in high school and you want that back again, make it your goal to get a visible six-pack, not just to just "get back in shape" which is a matter of opinion rather than something you can factually verify.

2. Decide what the "win" is in your system. If you are trying to expand your consulting business by 10 percent next month through calling your list, determine how many calls you'll have to make to land the clients. If you feel you will get those clients by the end of the month by calling for an extra hour each day, make that hour the win. It's not whether you land a new client each day, it's whether you put in the time. Over time, the system will do the work. Your small wins will add up to your desired outcome in due time.

3. Find the first step toward your win. For example, many people find that the first step to getting into the gym is to put on their gym clothes. Likewise, the first step to eating better may be to not buy unhealthy food. Start at the end, find your beginning, and fill in the intermediate steps.

4. Be prepared for the big win, your desired outcome. Know the next move after your desired outcome. Don't wait until you get there. If your business goal is to turn over $100, 000 per month and you hit it, how will you increase cash flow from it? Add on new steps to your system, or devise a new one that is more appropriate for your new situation. Vision is key for continued success.

Chapter 4
WINNERS ARE WARRIORS

Bobby Creighton should have played baseball. He was tall, but he was thin. He could hit, but he couldn't score. He was too young, but the boys loved him. Management thought he'd grow into his size and the coach admired his will to battle. This is why he stuck around so long after camp.

Though training camps end in August, junior teams' real training sessions begin in September. The worst part of this ninth month is that the practices last two hours. In March, before playoffs, you would be off the ice in an hour, ninety minutes tops. However, in September, the extra time is never wasted. In Regina, our team was no different.

Our coach's whistle cut through our hollow arena. It was cavernous, 5000 empty seats staring down at you from 100 feet above. Any word that was spoken reverberated through the steel girders and bounced back down to the ice. The only one who got to speak was the coach.

"Line up on the goal line," he said, tucking his whistle away. The calmer he said it, the worse you knew it was going to be. The bag skate was coming.

Somebody once asked me why conditioning drills are called a bag skate. The description gets lost right in name. It means to skate the bag out of you, to empty you—to skate you and skate you and skate you nonstop until you are doubled over, out of breath and seeing stars. No matter how tired you are, you don't want to be the slowest guy in your group to skate these lengths of the ice. It's not just pride. The last place guy has to skate the lengths again, alone. This makes everybody skate faster, so instead of working as a group to pace yourselves you turn on each other. Some hotshot at the front will take off so fast that his jersey looks like a hero's cape. You loathe him for that second. Your teammates become your enemies during a bagger, but the coach will call it "pushing each other" to perform better. That push was necessary. They needed to see your emotional depth in September. That's when the final cuts are made.

"Goal line and back. Shelly, your line," the coach said and blew his whistle.

Being a goalie, I always skated with the last line. I was put with the scratches, the guys who only played every second game. Bobby was one of these players. I looked down the goal line at Shane and Nate. Shane was slow and the most out of shape, but you had to be aware of him. Guys like Shane surprise you. They'll often work the hardest. They don't want to come last because then they have to skate again, even though they need it most. Nate was small and swift. He'd leave you bent over in his blazes, finishing first. Then there was Bobby. Lanky and lean, yet determined. Bobby was a skinny kid with a big head—Bobble Head.

When you're on the brink of getting cut, every inch counts. That one lost bag skate, that one minute being late, that one pass you missed. The rink is a petri dish and the coach looks down on you like a mad scientist trying to figure out the right formula for his team. The newspaper called our coach "Dr. Evil." He was bald, had piercing eyes and would incinerate your dreams if you disrespected his theories. I loved him. He had bred winners before.

As the first group of players blazed past, the coach coolly glided to the bench. He only needed to blow his whistle once. As each line returned, the next would know to go, each player cheating the line like a chuck wagon pony trying to get ahead of the start. The next line could start toward the far end of the ice when the first player from the previous line returned. This meant that after forty-five minutes some out of shape sucker would be getting half-lapped. That sucker would be singled out.

If you wanted to play in this league, the WHL, the top league in Western Canada, you had to see that physical punishment like this wasn't punishment at all. It was simply the way. You had to accept it as part of the job and power through it. When we took it, the coach always leaned against the boards and just observed. Your lower back tightened so much that you skated like an eighty year-old man walks. You couldn't bend over if you tried. Your legs would have searing heat spikes shoot through them before they would bake into bricks. The muscle couldn't release the blood. That blood stuck in your legs while your lungs struggled to hold oxygen into your body. The organ that lost out was your brain, and you'd get light-headed. It was a daze. No completed thoughts. A mess.

You always took solace in knowing that the rest of the boys were feeling that same pain as you. You were in it together. Hunched over, sticks across their knees, they were leaning on them so hard that they bowed. Standing straight got you more air, but your lungs would run wild. I hated this feeling. I didn't want to be the first one hunched over.

And don't you dare be that guy, the coward who takes a knee to keep from falling.

I looked down the goal line as our group rested after its fourth lap. Everybody still trying to put on a brave face. Nobody made eye contact with anybody else. If you didn't acknowledge another man's pain he wouldn't acknowledge yours. There would be no weakness shown. Egos preserved, partnerships binding.

I had heard of worse bag skates. An old teammate of mine once told me of how a now-NHL coach made his players do ninety minutes of non-stop skating, ten minutes for each goal they gave up, after a nine to two loss. He had all sorts of tricks that junior coaches can get away with where pros can't. Another time, he called a 5 a.m. practice after a particularly bad loss; sat on the bench for an hour and just read the newspaper. The players, dressed in sweat-soaked, cold gear from the night before had to just stand and watch, or so the folklore goes. He said that if the team was going to waste his time, he was going to waste theirs. He was also the most respected coach not only in the league at that time, but also in the whole country. I wish I could have played for him.

By about the twentieth time our line made the trip to the end boards and back, my stomach hurt. A pain curdled inside of me and was ripping at the inside of my ribcage. Behind me in the corner Bobby was the first one to take a knee. I feared for him. I liked Bobby. Everybody liked Bobby. Showing this weakness was one of those microscopic reasons for the coach to cut you at this time of year.

Our group left as the last one returned. Shane, Nate and I kicked our legs back, not able to bend at the knees, and made our way down the ice. As I banged my stick on the end boards, as customary so the coach knows you've touched it, I immediately turned to look back at Bobby. He was still on his knee. If he stayed down longer we'd all likely have to skate. My thoughts bounced from compassion to disdain as I reached home again.

"Bobble, get up," one of the vets called out. "Come on, kid!"

Bobby began retching. He heaved and heaved until a puddle of yellow Gatorade puke trailed from his mouth down in front of his knee. He stayed on his hands and knees and just stared into the puddle as more came. I was shocked. I stood straight and looked to Shelley at my left. He shrugged. The coach glanced over but said nothing. Our line left for another drag down the ice. Bobby stayed behind. *How could they skate us until we puked?* I thought. Everybody seemed to want to just not finish last in their group. There was no compassion. I turned back to head home again.

There was a figure making his way up ice alone—thin and withered, yet it was still moving. We crossed paths. It was Bobby. You could hear his skates carve through the snow-powdered ice and echo through the rink. A lone "Thatta boy, Bobble Head," came from the goal line. We finished the skate, and the coach gave us all the next day off...and by battling like a warrior, Bobby Creighton earned the right to hand out Gatordes on the bus after our first win of the year.

Being a Warrior

Warriors are winners. A Japanese proverb says: "Fall down seven times; stand up eight." I've heard this saying to the point of it being clichéd. Sayings like these are so overused that today's man is infatuated with the *idea* of getting up on the eighth time he's knocked down. He wants to *feel* like he's embracing the warrior spirit but does not actually go through the warrior's trials.

For example, the most respected players in a dressing room are the ones who battle through injuries in the playoffs. At the end of every season when a team has been eliminated, the whole dressing room knows which players have been playing with separated shoulders or bruised ribs and bad hips. Guys eat this up. The *idea* of being a warrior appeals to men. The act of slaying an opponent in battle or coming out as the underdog victor plays off the masculine need to thrive on challenge. The problem with modern men today is that we lack real challenges, so we are weakening. In hockey, we understand the sacrifice necessary for success on the ice. However, most men aren't translating that into their lives off the ice. Society glorifies the spoils of the battle, not the battle itself. Everybody wants the toys, not the lessons that earn them. It's time to start valuing what it takes to build a winner, not the prizes a winner gets.

Winners are built through battles, and we are what we repeatedly do. The mental strength to be a winner is not made from heroic gasps only when somebody is watching and through one-off moments of glory. Those specific points in time are just the culmination of work done over and over and over. The end win, the result everybody sees, comes from habits that have formed over time, mental habits. In my story above, Creighton battled through his pain not because he had a single heroic moment—trust me, no one has the energy to be a hero in a bag skate— but because he had been through many battles and held strong before. The war can't be won in the last battle if you didn't win the battles prior to that. All of the days of training, getting out of bed when you don't want to, those are the struggles where the seeds of winning are planted.

As a man, you need to start valuing the journey more than the destination, the process more than outcome. Although the spoils of a victory are rewarding when reached, the true lessons are learned on the way to them. The real win is learning how to wage war, and when you learn that, then the results pour in. When you chase a new purpose, even if you fail you will come away with new skills, new outlooks, and most importantly, new strength of mind. A man who has been through a battle before may still fear battle, but he also understands battle. He knows what he is getting into and he has built the confidence to handle it. This confidence endures because previous battles have built up his core essence. Since the masculine, that essence of being male and embracing the male polarity, thrives on challenge, the only way to grow it is to face new challenges. Even if you face the challenge and fail, you still gain skills and confidence in the process that can be used on your future or overarching purpose(s). You are training yourself to win.

This is why hockey is such a valuable tool for young men. It is the artificial war of modern society. Out on the ice, when two men are chasing down a loose puck or battling in the corners, they are building the resolve to not lose. When a team of junior players lines up on the goal line and gets bag skated, the resolve to not quit on your teammates builds up this strength too. These battles build mental strength.

Men have understood this for centuries. This includes tribal societies, Greco-Roman society, and even medieval apprenticeship. However, one of the most tremendous examples comes a little over a century ago—the Klondike gold rush of the 1890s.

When gold was struck in the Yukon, men from all over the world set sail for Alaska to trek the mountains into Canada in hope of striking it big. Rickety ships left daily in a race from Seattle, Washington north to Skagway, Alaska. After surviving the trip, men would buy 500 pounds worth of supplies to haul over a mountain pass in the dead of winter. This would take them three or four trips, if their supplies didn't get stolen. Then they'd camp until spring when the Yukon River broke up and raft toward the gold fields. Less than half of the more than 100, 000 men who made the trip to the Yukon made it this far. Less than half of those surviving men became miners. From that point, less than one per cent of miners struck gold, and less than 100 became legitimately rich. For most men, after risking their life savings and putting in a year of intense, high-risk labor, the only income they made was from selling their claim for pennies before they left.

Hearing this story, it may seem like one full of loss. Less than one per cent of men received any tangible results, but few regretted it. Overwhelmingly, most miners said the high point of their life was chasing the gold over those few short years. For many, it led them on a world of adventure. This expanded their comfort zone. For others, it broke down their fear of going broke (or starving or freezing.) Many cited it as the most courageous thing they ever did and would do it over again for the experience. They came for the gold, but they left irreversibly stronger for the rest of their lives. The battles in the experience turned them into warriors for the remainder of their lives and for their next purpose.

As a man, you need to give yourself experiences that challenge you. A good place to start is to find things that you fear and challenge them. Then stick with them, every day, especially when you don't want to stick with them. That is where your warrior's strength will be built for bigger wins.

Exercise

To build up your mental strength, you need shake yourself out of your typical consciousness. Use the exercise below to find a new challenge:

1. Think of one activity you've been putting off or would like to do but haven't. This is an ongoing activity, not just a one-off weekend. Write it down.
2. Pick a length of time you would like to devote to this activity.
3. Add twenty per cent more time than you originally chose.
4. Create a list of excuses you could use day-to-day to not complete that activity. You will have a list of excuses you know are invalid now. Add to it as you go.
5. Devise a system that will get you to do your activity every day. Go back to Chapter 2 if you need to.
6. Within the next two days, find a way to begin your activity. Do not worry if you are unprepared. Just start. This will force you to become prepared for the battle.

Chapter 5
WINNERS EMBRACE ACCOUNTABILITY

Phil was different than the other coaches. He didn't play their games. I liked that.

See, some coaches are tacticians. They'll draw diagrams that rival the battle plans of Napoleon. Others are yellers. When you do well, they yell. "That's a great fucking job out there," and then everybody in the room knows it. When you screw up, they yell too. "What the hell was going through your head out there?" Or the alternative, "Was your head up your ass?" Everybody down the hallway can hear it. But Phil was different.

With a long red moustache like Lanny MacDonald and the dark tan cowboy boots to match, Phil didn't yell much. Sometimes he'd pull out a marker to draw a forecheck or power play on the board, but his systems were straightforward. A peewee team using the room after us could have applied them. Our team needed that. Phil kept it simple. That was his style.

Unfortunately—for Phil and the rest of us—he didn't have a big budget with which to work. Budget is important in junior hockey. If you have some cash, you can build a nice dressing room for players, take long scouting trips to find true talent, and buy the players new gear each season. All of these necessities give coaches recruiting power, and good recruits create winning teams. Our budget was the smallest in the league.

We were playing against a rival team, one that was fighting with us for the last playoff spot. Like so many of my teams, we weren't winners. We'd come together as a team, win a couple of games, then completely fall out of sync, forget our systems and get totally outplayed. It was still happening in our last game of January.

That game, like so many, started out rough for all of us. Little errors sprung early. Defensemen made turnovers, forwards wouldn't dump the puck, line changes were too long. By the end of the first period, we were outshot about fifteen to four. I wasn't really surprised. Neither was Phil.

"Men, we're doing it again. We're doing it to ourselves again," Phil said, pacing our cramped room. Each thought was punctuated with a stop and a turn in the other direction. "I don't know why we do this to ourselves. You are better than this. You're giving them chances. This should be a closer game." The thing with Phil's lectures was that he could always point out the obvious—us losing—but our vets never embraced the corrections. It annoyed me. Our team needed leaders we didn't have.

Along the back wall, our leading scorer, Gilley, leaned back in his stall having a chew. You could have thrown him in a lawn chair at the lake. Phil's words left him glazed over, bored. Our young rookie, Jeff MacIntyre, put his head in his hands and stared at the floor, dreaming of playing at some higher level I was sure. The captain of this crew, Fuller, looked at Phil as he talked. He cared more than anybody, but he was also just a third liner. This team was a salty recipe for disaster—three lines of checkers, one line of pure prima-donna finesse. Mix and serve.

Personally, I took it all in stride. I got to play often, which in itself was a nice reward after riding the bench for two seasons. Routinely, I received forty shots per game, which was about twenty more than the goalie at the other end. If I didn't bring my A-game, we didn't have a chance. I knew this, Phil knew this, and the team knew this. That's why I really didn't get blamed in losses yet got champion status in wins. I was literally an all-star with a losing record.

"This isn't fair to our goalie. We can't leave Olie out to dry, boys," Phil said. "We've worked all week on a game plan for these guys. Let's use it this period. What do you say?" That was Phil—an optimist. He tried to bring us up instead of scare us up. Where other coaches would have kicked a water bottle at Gilley or got right up in MacIntyre's face, Phil just encouraged us. Personally, I kept my sanity while seeing guys slumping by focusing on what I could control—my game. Goalies are the quiet ones anyway.

I switched ends for the second period and looked at the clock behind me. Visitors – 2, Home – 0. If we could pop one early, we'd be back in the game. If I let in another, this game was likely another for the L column. The puck dropped and we won the draw. Our d-man, Chester, picked it up…and promptly turned the puck over for a two-on-one.

When Chester made that turnover, their winger barreled down the wall for a slapper. I got a piece of that two on one and put the rebound to the corner. Chester got beat to it and they set up in our end. After losing all battles to clear the puck, they put it past me in a scrum. I remember the sequence vividly—shot, save, rebound, save, rebound, pass, save, rebound, pass, save, rebound, goal. Four saves in about ten seconds before they scored. It felt like all ten guys on the ice were against me. One more goal later that period and they yanked me. We ended up losing six-nothing.

When you get pulled from a game, you do a little dance. You get to the bench, throw down your gloves and rip off a four-letter word under your breath. Then you stir in your sweat-soaked gear as the whole crowd looks down on you. Usually this is quite real. Getting pulled is no joke. When a forward gets benched, he blends in with eleven others. When a goalie gets pulled, the whole game stops. The announcer says who the new goalie is. Everybody watches you make the dreadful glide off the ice, tapping the new goalie's/victim's pad when you meet at center. You end this recall with an awkward shuffle around the gate, doing it in your oversized pads for added emphasis. It sucks.

On this night I was particularly pissed. I was more mad at our team than myself. I had learned a few lessons over the years. I was prepared. I had a system. I felt ready to win. Getting pulled was a serious offence to me. You can't explode on the team though, not every night. You win together, you lose together. I threw down my gloves and sat silently. The rest of the boys felt embarrassed enough as it was. We slinked off the ice at the game's end. Devastation in front of the home crowd.

After the game, showered and suited up, I stopped at Phil's office, an expanded storage closet, down the hall. He had said he wanted to talk to me. I figured he wanted to reassure me that I was hung out to dry and that he pulled me to spark the team.

"What happened to you out there tonight?" Phil said, from behind his desk. He leaned back in the pilot's chair, looking across at me.

"I got pulled—"

"Why?"

I felt a head game coming on. I'd seen these for a couple of years and I didn't want to deal with it. Phil didn't play head games and I respected that.

"We needed to give the team a spark," I said.

"A spark? You think we needed a spark, eh," Phil said. "I'll tell you what kind of spark we needed. We needed you out there. We can't expect to win if you don't play. You didn't fill your role. When you don't come to play, we lose."

"Phil, I stop four shots in a row and let in the fifth. Where is the rest of the team?"

Phil shot up. He leaned over his desk, his eyes growing wider.

"Your job is to stop the fifth, and the sixth and the tenth. I don't care. We need you to do that. You're *our* guy."

"But Phil," I said. "I get forty shots every night. Nobody else in the league gets that many shots. How do you expect me to win?"

"One-nothing, two to one, I don't care. There are nights when I need you to stop all forty. *We* need you to stop all forty. You want this job? That's the requirement. Think about if you still want it."

"Okay," I said. That was that. I left his office and drove home in shock.

Winding down after a game was always tough for me. My brain would replay the game in the darkness of my bedroom. My lungs would be relaxed but the oxygen would be blasting through my blood. I often couldn't pass out until 2 a.m. Instead, I'd lie on the couch, zone out and watch TV infomercials until I fell asleep right there.

As I lay there, Phil's rant rattled in my ears. It stood out. It was so different. Usually, he wasn't so direct, so clear. Most times his message was a muttered, "You guys gotta play better," and "We can't keep playing like this." I couldn't tune out his words.

I was right. It wasn't fair that I should be the one who gets yelled at in a loss when the whole team doesn't show up to play. Tough shit, I thought in remorse. That's being a goalie. I lay there meditating. Thinking. No matter how I tried to slice it, I may have been right that it wasn't fair that I shoulder the loss. However, Phil made a stronger point—it didn't matter what the rest of the team did. If we were going to turn into a winner I'd have to start accepting responsibility, win or lose. I'd have to be accountable. Where excuses could be made, I'd have to find a way to win instead. Our opponents would not let up. I'd have to play better than the other goalie every night, even if I received double the shots. That's what it would take to win. I wanted to be a winner. I'd have to find a way.

The next day we had practice. The jaded veterans showed up as late as possible. The hopeful rookies hit the ice just ahead of the veterans. As the most veteran guy, I went out with the rookies and warmed-up early. Phil ran a light practice, the kind that you love late in the season—quick warmup, power play work and take the rest of the day off to recover. We still had the ice booked after and it was optional to do what we liked. I may have been an old, jaded veteran, but I didn't leave early after practice. I got the rookies to stay out and shoot on me long until everybody left the rink. I had to stop when I was doubled over trying to catch my breath after the drill. I looked up and through the glass. Phil passed on his way out. No smile, no response, just a knowing look from him.

Phil kept it simple, and Phil started me the next game. After all, I was our starting goalie.

Taking Accountability

A winner knows he creates his own greatness. In his mind, he is responsible for his outcomes—good or bad.

In the coaching side of my business, the Junior Hockey Truth, I often get hockey parents who come to me and say, "Johnny is a great player. I know he can make it, but this, that and the other are all unfair things working against him. I know it's not his fault, but…" I feel bad for Johnny in these cases because it is clear that his parents are making excuses for him. What they are telling Johnny is that it is not his fault if he doesn't make it. However, if Johnny did "make it" would it also not be by his own doing? That attribution is key. Being judicial about this attribution comes from being accountable.

Being accountable means that you can be relied upon to follow through on your purpose in any situation. This purpose can be your life's greatest purpose, your role when working with others, or even keeping yourself honest on a project. You need to be accountable for your results and understand that you determine them. Hockey creates classic examples of this.

How many times have you seen an underdog team upset a league leader? The first thing that league leader's captain will say after the game is, "We didn't show up to play. We did this to ourselves."

Ironically if the underdogs lose, their captain would echo the same sentiment. He'll say, "We knew they were a good team and we weren't prepared." Captains at the highest level do this because they don't want to give away their power, their ability to change their own fate. The same strength that lies in saying, "Look, it may not have been fair out there, but fair doesn't matter. We didn't find a better way," is the precursor to, "We worked hard for this all year long. Every guy in this room deserves it." By being accountable for how you perform in life, you enable yourself to perform better. It's self-empowerment. The man who recognizes his faults in losses is the man who has the courage to win. Yet, recognition is not enough.

In this chapter's story, I needed to redeem my role as starting goalie. I liked being the hero on the nights I'd stop forty shots and we'd win. On the nights we'd lose, I wouldn't always hold myself accountable for those losses. I could say I was part of the team and had to play better next time, yet I'd silently think it wasn't my fault, that I was hung out to dry. I only took responsibility for the goals that were my fault, even though it was a team game and I was a member of the team. Then I'd go back the next game, resting on my laurels as one of the top goalies on a bad team, repeating the losing process. I never did anything to alter my ego until Phil had that talk with me. Being accountable is taking action so the mistakes of the past aren't repeated. It's not avoidance of action. I only started seeing success when Phil taught me this lesson about accountability.

That's a key difference between winners and losers. The winners admit change is in their power and do what it takes to find solutions so losses don't occur again. True losers don't accept responsibility and closet-losers do one worse—they admit responsibility yet never alter their actions. They know they have a problem to deal with, yet they silently hope the problem goes away and try to avoid it. They never do anything about it! That's like telling the other team the only way you can win is if they play worse than you.

Every year around the Christmas holidays there are plenty of clear examples of people not accepting responsibility. Have you gathered for family dinners and drinks, gorged on food, gained five pounds and then said, "Jeez, I gotta go to the gym in the new year!" If you have done this but keep doing it every year, you're losing. Making excuses that it's the holiday season will not prevent you from getting fatter. Many people will go to the gym as a New Year's resolution, which is a good thing. However, ninety-five percent of people also quit their resolutions by January fifteenth. If you stuff the food into yourself, go to the gym for a week and never return, you're not learning, especially when you do it year after year. Having a winning system in place for not overeating over the holidays could solve this problem, and if you slip up, you'd have an easy way to be accountable—go to the gym year-round. Being accountable to your body lets you get back on your feet in this case.

Responsibility is easy to accept, but being accountable is tougher. If you find yourself in an unfortunate circumstance, you must examine how you got there. There is always something you could have done to change that circumstance. You're the director of your life, not a spectator. Being accountable requires you to not only admit you made a mistake, but also to make it real—you have to take action to prevent it from happening again. Your ego will trip up at this point. It will look for excuses and find people and circumstances to blame. When I find myself in this position, I like to remind myself that somebody else out there is finding a way around the same problem by being accountable. I know there is a way if I want it bad enough. If being accountable forwards me on my purpose, it's a no-brainer to accept responsibility for my actions and then to act on that decision.

At the same time, I can use the principle of accountability to build confidence in my wins. Whenever I achieve something great, I always break it down to discover the process—the system—that led to the event. That way I can repeat it and know it was by my own doing. Circumstances may seem incidental when you reach success, but if you can replicate those circumstances, you can predict your success again and again.

Exercise

Recognizing what outcomes are truly in your power to change and which ones you can alter in the future are learned skills. The formula below will help you discover why events in your life occur—fortunate or unfortunate. Right now, use the formula below to break down what led to a win or a loss in your life that happened today:

1. In the steps leading up to your outcome, identify the turning point that made the event happen.
2. From the turning point in step one, work backward to the first point in time where you could have taken control of the situation and shaped it in your favor.
3. When you find that moment in step two, identify your mindset or actions at the time. How did it help or hurt you?

4. Replace that mindset or action with a new, more advantageous one. For instance, if you got into a car accident because you were texting and driving, what would you do different next time? Not text, of course. Your new mindset/action in the future would be not allowing yourself to text and drive.

5. Create an affirmation you can tell yourself when the trigger you've identified comes up again. For our texting example, simply saying to yourself, "Texts can wait until I stop. If it is important they will answer my reply later." You can use that affirmation next time you feel the trigger event coming on. Changing your actions at that point will alter the outcome down the line.

Chapter 6
WINNERS HAVE MENTORS

W hen you're a WHL goalie, you're one of the top forty goalies from thousands in Western Canada. You haven't made it yet, but you've made it somewhere. There is some level of respect with it. However, within your dressing room, you're just one player in a herd.

Every time you move up to another level, the teammates you played with get left behind. You need to keep developing. I felt I had stopped developing at eighteen. It seemed the game wasn't getting any easier for me. I had achieved more in hockey than ninety-nine per cent of players I'd ever played against as a kid. But that last per cent was the toughest. I had been cut from the WHL once before by the Regina Pats, dropped entirely, and fought my way back on with another team, the Tri-City

Americans. Something felt wrong with my game and I couldn't find the root of the problem.

When a player snuck down on the back-door, I'd drop to my knees too quickly. When a defenseman let a cannon rip from the point, I'd drop to my knees too quickly. When a wily little centerman came in alone, I'd drop to my knees too quickly. I had one big problem. Stand up, right? Seems simple, right? Not the case. Not in that split-second time for reaction.

Ever since I was a kid, maybe nine or ten years old, I was told I was big, that I covered lots of net. And at eighteen, I was about six-foot-four, so the evidence was there. I was always told that I was a "butterfly goalie" and that on my knees I still covered the top half of the net. I believe that I could be a wall out there if I had the angle. I'd drop on every shot. This strategy worked until I played junior. Guys just go around you when you drop to your knees in junior.

I tried standing up more, but it was uncomfortable. My modus operandi was to put my shins parallel to the ice, slam my knees together and fan my feet out. Standing up, while conventionally sound advice, was hard to implement. Thousands and thousands of times I'd dropped. When a future NHLer comes in on you, you can't break that habit on the spot.

In practice, I caught shit. I tried breaking the habit by standing up more, but it looked like I wasn't trying. A winger would cut in off the wall on a two-on-one and I'd try to stay on my feet. He'd slide it low. Somebody would yell from the corner, "Hey Olie, sleep at night bud." I must have looked in a daze. I'd start dropping again with mediocre success.

After one of these stand and drop practices, I found a letter in my stall. I figured it was a sales pitch for some elite service—I wasn't of the fan letter quality—that should be thrown away. Yet, it had the word "goaltending" in the return address, so I figured that was worth a look.

I didn't know the man who wrote it would change my game. Below its typical business-letter letterhead, it said something to this effect:

Dear Nick,

As a member of the Western Hockey League, you are an ideal candidate for our elite training program. I am a goalie coach for another team in the WHL and I help goalies take their game to the next level during the off-season. Please call me soon and I can help take you to the next level too.

Sincerely,

Mike

I stripped off my gear in a hot steamy pile, showered and organized my stall. As I threw on my jacket, I saw the torn envelope in my stall. Letters like these were common. Some goalie coach who was the best show in his city would send out a mass mailer. Their logos were some silhouetted goalie with gear that looked like it survived the '72 Summit Series. The company name invariably had "elite" or "pro" in the name: World Elite Goaltending, Pro Elite Goaltending. That kind of thing. I took the letter home with me to put in my pile.

As I put the letter in my drawer of junk, I gave it a second read-over. I got letters often, but not *that* many.

What's the harm in calling? I thought, later that night. I picked up the phone.

"Hi, this is Mike."

"Hi, Mike. This is Nick Olynyk from the Tri-City Americans. I received your letter in the mail today."

"Nick, nice to hear from you. How are things in Tri-City?"

Mike and I talked for a half-an-hour. I'd never heard of him before, but he'd been training goalies for over a decade. Without saying it, he seemed to have a knack for helping high-level goaltenders, judging by the pros he'd taught. When I asked questions, he listened. When we talked about the position, he was engaged. Mike loved goaltending.

Within a week, Mike and I worked out a deal. I'd work a load of his goalie camps during the day. He'd teach me at night. That summer would change everything.

I arrived at Mike's camp, pads buckled together over my shoulder, in July. He went over the itinerary with me and a couple other junior goalies. Every day we would do work on skating, then we would do drills on "reading the puck." Reading the puck means knowing where it's going to be shot before the shot hits you. You "track" the puck all the way in as you *react* to it. Other goalie coaches at the time preached a blocking style, dropping to your knees and being a wall that slide back in forth like a table hockey goalie. Mike's methods were different. They were innovative for their time.

Now, I got the basics of goaltending—skating, reading the puck, etc. I'd learned the basics when I was in novice, and now as a junior I'd teach them back to novice kids. This camp required me to teach eight hours per day. After that, we, the instructors all in junior, hit the ice for two hours in the evening to do skating and movement drills. It was exhausting and so…basic. I wasn't convinced.

After a few customary laps around the ice and some stretching, the handful of us took to far end of the rink to start.

"Who wants to go first?" Mike said, leaning back on his elbow at the crossbar. One after another, I watched some of the best prospects in the province skate T's and X's and W's around the crease. They'd push the net off its moorings from clinking the posts so much. These guys were fast. They transitioned so well. They also were either younger than me or playing at a lower level. I took to the net thinking I'd show them a thing or two. You always want to step up as the oldest guy.

I made a quick sprint from my post out of my crease and dug my toe in for a quicker stop. It felt like I was pulling a semi trailer as my toes and heels drilled down into the ice with my now six-foot-five frame. I went back to the post and out to the middle… and went ass over tea kettle. Nobody laughed. It was more shock. The oldest guy at the highest level couldn't do the novice drill. For the next thirty minutes we did more of these drills. Consistently, I struggled. It was embarrassing. I slammed my stick on the ice at the final one as everybody went for a cool down lap. Mike skated beside me.

"What did you think of that?" he said to me.

"I, I think…" I was huffing and puffing. "I think I got some work to do."

"Look, you're a big goalie. You have a ton of advantages other guys don't have. We're going to work with you every day on your skating until you tear the ice down to the blue paint. Big guys need better footwork and you'll get it."

I sure hoped so.

For the next two weeks, Mike paid particular attention to my skating. Everyday my hips and back would burn and turn into solid granite by the time I finished the drills. My pads would feel like they weighed a ton. I also got quicker. It was a major eye-opener.

That fall I went back to Tri-City. For the most part, I had a solid training camp. I felt smooth and in control of my game. The shots seemed to move at a slower speed and I was meeting them square. I was no longer dropping without reason and felt control in my game. As we went through exhibition, I got a shutout over our rivals, Spokane. The team even mounted the puck for me on a plaque. I owe that one to Mike.

Finding a Mentor

Nothing can fast track your learning and skill development more than learning from somebody who has already made the mistakes. As a man who is seeking to improve himself, you're going to require mentors to help you on your purpose. Ironically, the way to get a mentor to help you is for you to help them. You need to offer them value. However, before you can make an offer, you need to know what kind of mentor you want.

As you can see in my story, a mentor (or mentorship) doesn't have to be somebody close. When I say the word mentor, some men conjure images of an old bearded man in a wood shop teaching a young apprentice how to carve. Mentors come in more ways than you'd traditionally think. You can find *mentor*ship in a variety of ways: books like this one, seminars, training, coaching and volunteering are all ways of gaining mentorship. The idea of having somebody purposefully take you under their wing—while good—is just one way.

Of course, the big question is: how do you find a mentor? My favorite answer to this is an old saying: "Closed mouths don't get fed." If you want mentorship, you have to seek it out. My best mentors have come from me contacting them first and showing appreciation and service. Oftentimes people who are in a position to be great mentors are low on time. Everybody wants a piece of them, and they are just keeping their heads above the waves of demands on their time. This is actually a great thing for you.

If you can identify what a potential mentor needs by way of help, you can offer that. This can separate you from others. In turn, you'll be close to that mentor and receive their guidance. For some of my online business, I've mentored under a couple of different people who were tops in their industries (always look for the *top* people.) After getting an introduction to my first mentor from a friend, I actually scraped up what was left of my savings in university and flew to meet him. Impressed with my zeal and ability to add value, he invited to join him again later that summer at another one of his training sessions. This became an ongoing theme and I got to follow him around the world as he conducted seminars. I did little things like get coffee and direct attendees throughout the weekend, but doing these things took some of the burden off of him. It added value. And the more value I added, the more he helped me and introduced me to *his* people. Back home, when I needed marketing advice, he was just an email away or could point me in the right direction. It saved me hours of pain just being able to click "send" when I had a question. I skipped the trial and error by just asking what the error was without the trials.

It's no different than when I worked with Mike. Mike showed me that I was a half-second behind the play because my balance was off. Remember how I fell ass over tea kettle when doing basic drills in the story above? That's because I was leaning too far forward, only a matter of inches. That little shift may seem too basic, even unbelievable, for a guy playing at a high level of junior hockey. However, often when you're trying to break through to a new level, it's those little shifts you can't notice. They are so small, so seemingly inconsequential that we don't even see them. The coach or mentor, he or she sees them every day. It's that coach's job to find the little shifts. Your job is to find the right coach.

A good mentor has a solid track record of success. While a resume of experience is good, a resume of experience and coaching is better. For example, Wayne Gretzky is undeniably the greatest hockey player ever. Yet, he had a tough time coaching. On the other hand, Scotty Bowman is the winningest coach of all-time. He played the game at a decent level, but moreover he's coached at a higher standard than anybody ever has. If I'm looking for a coach of the next Stanley Cup champions, I'm choosing Scotty Bowman.

Secondly, your mentor doesn't have to have the same perfect beliefs you have. They only have to have the ones you want in the area you're looking to improve. For example, one of my first business mentors was a great guy but was in poor physical shape. He had the syndrome of never leaving his computer chair and it took a toll on his body. One of my beliefs is that you need to be solid physical shape to get the most out of your day. He didn't endorse this belief. However, when it came to teaching my Internet business, I didn't care. The knowledge in that particular area served me well, so I listened. You only need your beliefs to connect in the area in which you're working (and even then they don't have to be perfect.) It may even be wise to not adopt every belief of your mentor.

It's also worth noting that you have to keep the right perspective on mentorship. Before you approach a potential mentor, ask yourself, "What can I offer?" The mentor needs value from you or else you're a drain on them. Don't confuse this with, "I need skills to offer." The whole reason you're seeking out the mentor is to improve your skills. What you need to show is a determination to learn through osmosis and the ability to give your effort before you expect anything in return. The old saying, "The teacher will appear when the student is ready," is appropriate. Your mentor will be more willing to teach you when he sees that your progress is helping him.

Last, you must seek out a mentor. You must ask. Be okay with hearing "No." Expect it. If you want to learn from somebody better than you, you may have to find more than one person who is better than you. Some mentors have people lining up around the block wanting to learn from them. You simply won't be able to reach others. They'll just be too far up the ladder. There will, however, be one mentor out there for you who is thrilled or even honored to be seen as a thought leader. They'll appreciate the gesture. You just have to remember that your job is to offer them something before they give something back.

If you can't find a mentor, don't have the time to search for one, or simply want to get the info you need faster, you can always pay for it. Books and seminars are great places to gain knowledge and make new connections. As long as you choose your materials as wisely as you'd choose your mentors, you'll be on the fast track to learning. Do what it takes to get the skills you need.

Exercise

These are the steps you can take to finding a solid mentor:

1. Identify what skill(s) you want to learn as they pertain to your purpose. If part of your system is not working, find the missing piece.

2. Find as much free info as you can about that skill. Before presenting yourself to a mentor, you want to show you have a hunger and some knowledge. Looking for free info also programs your brain to start thinking in line with what skill you need.

3. If you haven't come across a mentor in step two, start searching them out. Use Google, ask friends and your network. Put yourself out there. Mentors who need people don't always officially advertise it.

4. Do background research on your prospective mentor. Do they have solid reviews? Do you have referrals? Are they walking the walk? Also, get specific info on them so you're prepared to meet.

5. Approach the mentor with respect, show what you can offer, explain why you want to help them so they know what you want. Expect to give more than you receive.

6. Be okay hearing "no," and don't stopping asking others until you hear "yes."

Chapter 7
WINNERS LEARN BY DOING

Nick really pulled his weenie out of the fire on that one," the play-by-play man said, or so I was told after. I was in my second ever playoff game in the WHL. My weenie caught fire when I had stepped out of my net to play the puck, and promptly turned it over to Moose Jaw's forward. Before he could fire into the gaping cage, I dove back into the crease and the puck got lodged somewhere in my gut. Five thousand people collectively "ohhhed" at me. I was lucky. I never should have been in net to start with.

An optimist might have said the reason for my start was fate or perhaps a sign that I should play. A realist would state the obvious—our starting goalie was suspended for throwing his stick into the stands and clocking an old lady the game before. Playing for the Regina Pats that season, I didn't know who had a worse fate: me or that old lady.

I loved Regina, but we were horrible. The only thing that kept us in the playoff race was our other goalie, Dustin Slade. The kid was lightning fast and just as competitive. He also had a penchant for attention. A scout once told me that Slade had some of the best natural talent of a goalie he had ever seen…from the shoulders down. I haven't found a better description yet. Slade, "Dusty" as he signed all his autographs, had been suspended previously for blockering a Moose Jaw player in the face and skating the length of the ice to fight the other goalie. This wasn't a line brawl. He just decided to skate the length. The fans loved it, the management didn't mind it, and as for the media, the kid made it easy for them. Like the smartest eighth grader who comes to school just to goof off, Slade was our most talented player who trouble seemed to find. Moose Jaw knew this.

In the first game, they went straight for him. Everybody saw it coming. He had kept his blocker out of opponents' mouths for a solid month, but he just couldn't let this one go. After we cleared the zone, one of our defenseman got tangled up with a Moose Jaw forward in Slade's crease. He gave the guy a light nudge. The guy gave a push back. By the time the whistle went, the pushes turned to punches and Slade was ejected. On his escort off the ice—referee handoff to police for Slade's safety—he clocked a lady in the head, using his stick as a javelin. He launched that thing up a few rows before disappearing down the tunnel. With one minute remaining in the previous period, I knew I was going in to replace Slade for the rest of the series.

"You little shit. You little shit…" was the start of our coach's tirade as he burst into the room. Coaches rarely burst into the room. They save that for when they need to shock the team, but in this case he was enraged. Furious, tyrannical anger. Standing a foot away from Slade, the coach poked his finger right into Slade's chest. I could see the lightning in his eyes. "You said you would keep it together. You promised us…Take your fuckin' gear off. You're done. You're going to be done for the year."

A losing team is like a dysfunctional family. The head coach is the father. He is angry all the time and yells at his kids, the players, nonstop. The assistant coach, like the mother, tries to raise the kids up because the dad's already yelling at them. They need some encouragement. Usually, one of the older brothers, the best player on the team, does his job well enough that it keeps the family afloat…until he (i.e., Slade), gets in trouble with the father. Nobody prospers. In our scenario, I was that forgotten middle child with the gimpy leg. As the backup, I was always pushed to the back of the room, always the afterthought. Like the most classic of tales, getting thrown into this game was my chance to step up.

Coming off the bench is the worst in my opinion. Contrary to common clichés, as a benchwarmer you don't always sit on the bench in these junior rinks. Sometimes you stand behind it on skates, probably wearing wet gear from the morning skate. Sometimes you lean on the steel-framed door and swing it. Each period takes about forty-five minutes from the time you reach the bench to when you leave it, so it's not a short stint to stand. After one period my hands always froze and my toes would get numb. However, it was the best seat in the house in the best junior league in the world. And when I did get thrown in, it was the toughest opportunity to prove myself. As a backup goalie, you're happy to play, but it's always under the worst circumstances—a blowout score, an injury, your partner blockering a guy in the face and sticking an old lady in the melon. You can never show that you are happy to get thrown in either (because you're probably losing), and you're never fully ready for it (because you've been standing for two hours.). You're entering a sprint halfway through the race, cold. However, to be a winner, you can't whine and you can't make excuses. You have to go in and perform. The necessary result doesn't change.

I was excited, not nervous, to enter the net, kind of like a pony who finally gets let out of the barn. I had never expected to play another minute until the next season and now I had the chance. Ready or not, I took a little stretch, nodded at the ref and the game was back on. I knew I would play the game or the game would play me.

After winning the draw at center, the first thing Moose Jaw did was fire a long one down on me. Opponents always want to test a cold goalie early, catching him on his heels. The shot snuck through me and landed on the goal line. I thought it was just a fluke. By the end of the next game, back in Moose Jaw, my weenie was getting pulled out of the fire.

— — —

The next game when Moose Jaw's forward fired that shot at open net and I dove back in, I felt a shift. A couple months before, I would have thought I wasn't ready to play in a playoff game. I would have questioned if I belonged. I would have just played not to lose. When I dived to stop that shot though, I kept us in the game. I was doing my job. In fact, we were even winning. Every save I made grew my confidence. It was learning on the job at its finest.

But by the end of that game, we lost our lead. We were badly outshot. We couldn't hold it together. That's why we had to sneak into playoffs. The series spiraled out of control and we got swept in four games. I hated to see the Moose Jaw fans in our rink brandishing brooms, tapping them on the glass behind me in warm-ups. I didn't win a game. However, I did learn a valuable lesson about winning. Winners learn to handle pressure, and they only learn this by facing pressure. Through the boos and calls and doubters and negative prognosticators, I showed up each game. I did the best I could with what I had. Where sitting on the bench would have got me nowhere, facing the flames got me somewhere. Even in the losses and struggles, I gained the most valuable experience an unproven rookie backup could get: playing time. That's why, four years later, I had the privilege of being the starting goalie for the Vernon Vipers as we marched straight to the league finals. There were no games more pressure-filled than those, but they didn't seem that way. The pressure forced me to the top of my game, and I owe that to the experience of being in Regina. Playing as a backup at seventeen shot my progress ahead further than taking it slow and cautious would have. I learned to win by doing, even if I needed to lose a little at first.

Learning to Win

Winners are bred, not born. The process of rising to the top is one that must be learned. Everybody starts their season and their life at zero. From there you have to prove to yourself that you can win. To win, you must play the game.

For young men, a lack of belief is often due to a lack of action, and a lack of action is often due to a lack of belief. It can be a vicious circle. The man who never tries at anything is one who never wins at anything. You have to be willing to lose before you can learn to win.

And you lose you must. Wins get attention, but losses give lessons. A common question many personal development coaches ask is, "How fast are you willing to fail?" The more times you put yourself in the line of failure, the more lessons you learn. And if failing, on the surface, is a loss, you're simply learning what it takes not to win. Then you do the opposite.

As time goes on and your experience grows, you'll develop confidence. Your belief in your abilities grows and so do the contingencies you use to unlock those abilities. For instance, I had played in playoff games before the ones in my story above. That wasn't new to me. Playing in a *junior* playoff game was though, and I had to learn how to handle it as I went. There was no training course on how to play in games that intense; I had to get in some of them. We lost those games, and the lessons learned from them served me well later, when they mattered the most. If I had never played in those harsh games at seventeen in Regina, I certainly wouldn't have been ready for the harsher ones at twenty. My team at twenty needed me to be their guy, and I rose to that challenge. The failures I had thrown myself into early taught me the lessons I needed later. I needed to lose a few so I could learn how to win.

Whether it's being willing to lose or taking action because action is needed, as a man you can only learn to win at your purpose if you get on your purpose. Too many men are afraid to start chasing their true purpose because if they don't reach it they feel they are failures. Their ego stops them. That fear of failure keeps them in their comfort zone. Why face the potential pain of losing, after all? Obviously, achieving more would make you feel better in the long run, but your ego fights that fear in the short term. It always seeks to avoid pain. You have to be okay facing the pain of struggle and loss first in order to relish the rewards of winning later.

If you want to reach a new level of success in a current pursuit, or if you want to master a new one, you need to expose yourself to the flames of battle. I have many contacts of all ages who do different types of online marketing. Some of them are multi-millionaires, some of them are still learning the ropes. The common thread amongst all of them when I ask how they've reached the level they are at? They said you have to be willing to lose a few thousand at first as the cost of learning. Lose thousands now to make millions later—that's their mantra. Where I saw others fail was when they didn't have the capacity to endure the losses. In order to make the millions, these marketers had to lose $10, 000 first. It took that amount of losses for them to figure out the pictures, headlines, write-ups and thousands of other little factors that make those annoying ads in your sidebar work. Once they did that, they started making $500 to $1000 dollars per day. Rather than be content, they started new ad campaigns across different niches to learn more skills. They put himself in line for more losses. A year later, $500 to $1000 dollars per day was nothing. Soon, they had a team of hungry young learners working for them and they were borrowing everybody's credit cards so they could buy more ads. Some days they would spend five or even six figures to buy ads. A couple of these guys now have financial freedom at thirty. These are the guys who were willing to risk it all and endure initial losses.

The guys who invest one or two thousand and quit often start with a hope—a dangerous emotion—of striking it big, but they retreat at their first losses. Rather than expecting casualties on the way, they say screw it and quit. They want the purpose of freedom in their lives so they can do greater things, but they either stop at the fear of losing money or the fear of striking it big.

Being afraid of loss seems obvious, but some men also have a fear of winning. Once you become a winner, once you reach a higher level of success, you suddenly start molding your world into a winner's world. You are seen as a winner, you expect yourself to be a winner. When you go from playing on the third line in life and move up to the first because you start scoring, you should expect yourself to keep scoring. Your ego actually doesn't want this. Now you're not just expected to chip in a goal every once in a while, you're expected to do it every game. That's pressure and your ego doesn't want it. It's no different in life. Many men get on the path to success and start to adopt it as identity. Then if they lose the success—the contingency—they start to feel miserable. They forget they are the same man. Their ego makes them feel miserable because the man is not aligning to his new identity. It wants more wins and wins aren't easy. Having been along for small wins over time, a man's ego knows that with each win comes greater pressure. Many times, this ego will hold him back so he doesn't reach for the biggest wins. This same mechanism that keeps you from avoiding the pain of loss is also the same one that keeps you from avoiding potential pain after wins. The ego is a cowardly mechanism.

Knowing how this ego works, you must go out for your next game, prepared or not, and step in the crease. Do not be afraid of losing. You don't win as long as you try, you win because you are growing your comfort zone. The larger that grows, the greater the wins will be down the road. You're building your capacity for a greater purpose.

Exercise

Many men let the fear of loss or fear of success hold them back from bigger wins as they chase their purpose. Use the system below to identify how you can grow your comfort zone.

1. Ask yourself what is one major benchmark you'd like to achieve as you pursue your purpose. For example, if you have a purpose right now of getting in peak physical condition, it may be running your first marathon. That would be a benchmark that you are hitting the highest echelons of your fitness goals.

2. Identify as many reasons as possible for not being able to reach this benchmark. Write them down. Start with the fears of failure, then the fears of success.

3. Ask yourself what the first step to achieving your benchmark will be. List what you need to do to undertake that step TODAY. Every marathon starts with one step.

4. When you finish that first step, ask what the next one is. Have belief in the process, endure the losses, and you'll see yourself moving toward the wins.

Chapter 8
WINNERS ARE LEADERS

Ryp's cheek looked like he had a black and blue baseball implanted in it. The mass of blood-filled tissue swelled on his face left no question as to what had happened—one heck of an uneven fight.

Neither the biggest, nor the strongest player I had ever played with, Rick Rypien was one of the toughest and most courageous. Earlier that fall, we would drive to practice together. Sometimes the rides were quiet, and sometimes we'd talk. I was just a rookie and still hadn't made the Regina Pats. Rick was next in line to be team captain. He knew the ropes when I was just trying to grab on. I often didn't know what to say. Rick often didn't either, but he was a quiet kind of leader.

We had a bad team, really bad in fact. We were second-last in the league yet still made playoffs in our division—the last place team,

Saskatoon, pretty much set a record for worst season ever. The concept of winning was lost on us. Some nights the whole team would show up to play. This would give us a fighting chance at best. Most nights we didn't show up and lost, including the one where Rick got in the fight.

Rick's cheek was black and blue because he wouldn't back down. I saw it all from the other end of the ice. It was my second game ever, and without checking the score today, I know we lost (I didn't win a single game my first season.) We were playing Moose Jaw who had a handful of future NHLers. Our only future NHLer was Rick. I sat three stalls down from him.

"You know what happens to a light switch when you fuck with it?" our coach asked. "It fuckin' breaks.

"You play with it and play with it, and then you come one day and it won't turn on. You have to keep that switch on every game, guys."

The man would not go down without a fight, and Rick was his kind of leader.

"We got ahead and let them back into this one. I need all of you to show up this period," he said. "Ryp, your line is starting."

It was rare that we could keep up with Moose Jaw until the third period. They were pretty much tops in our division. They were also our bitter rivals. We played Moose Jaw ten times out of a seventy-two-game schedule, often back-to-back down the stretch.

Moose Jaw was also loaded with pricks. They would slash you on the back of the shins when the play left your end and their veterans would chirp you on the red line during warmup. One of their Euros even managed to knee me going through my crease late in the season. Consequentially, I tore the cartilage in my right knee and I am now missing half of it. It's a reminder of this rivalry every time a season changes, that ache from Moose Jaw that won't leave me.

Moose Jaw wasn't exactly a small team either, and very few of their guys stood less than six feet. One of these players towered above the rest on the blue line—Lane Manson. In the dressing room, we had a lot of names for Manson, the six-foot nine defenseman who could move well enough that the now defunct Atlanta Thrashers drafted him. However, few players would say any names to his face. They likely looked him in the chest anyway.

As we lined up for the opening faceoff of the period, I could see Manson tower in the background as the centers lined up for the faceoff. True to form, we lost the draw and things went downhill from there. Within three minutes, Moose Jaw scored a go-ahead goal on me. They repeated it two minutes after that. We entered the period in a tie, and we were down by two before anybody got a second shift. Turnovers, defensive breakdowns, questionable goaltending. We were giving away a chance to win. Nobody stepped up…except Rick.

After giving up the lead, Rick's line took the ice for a second time that period and he promptly scored. The thing I remember most about Rick's goals was that he battled to get every one. He'd chip away at you, give you the extra shove and take all sorts of abuse in front of the net to score. He was the kind of guy who the trainer would have to concoct some kind of foam cutout for to act as padding for his bruised ribs. He'd draw penalties taking so many crosschecks in front of the net. On this night, Manson was giving them to him. I remember that giant pushing Rick and pushing Rick, and Rick just planting himself and digging in. Many people remember Rick as an NHL fighter and role player, but in junior he was also a scorer. Some of the goals were pretty, but he often had to battle for those ugly ones. He battled his way to the NHL just like he was about to battle Manson.

Rick was the only one to step up and scored our only goal that period. He wanted to send a message. Moose Jaw was cocky. That ate at us and Rick was our quiet leader. At 19:55, he entered one last battle with Manson in the corner, and at 19:58 he dropped his gloves. The size difference looked like Andre the Giant versus a high schooler. Both stared each other down without flinching.

Rick raised his fists up, boxing style, as he trained. Manson spread his wider, staring over them, not through. With a lunge and a pounce they grabbed each other and cocked their fists, catching peeks every second to see if they could swing. Manson didn't throw a punch early. Rick started swinging. The crowd was amused—the light cheer of support from those left in the stands, the silence from those who could see the mismatch and how it would inevitably play out. Rick missed once, twice and Manson just held him out. A rag doll move. With an outstretched arm, Rick couldn't reach him. And that's when Rick shifted his weight and landed one big blow. Manson bounced back. You could see a shift in his shoulders. He started to take the fight seriously at that point. Rick fervently swung, and Manson, much too tall, leaned back and took a couple big swings, landing square on Rick's cheek.

You could see the wince—his head dropped for a second and his teeth clenched. That punch stung. But he bounced back. Swinging, swinging, swinging, and when he couldn't reach Manson's face he went for his ribs. Rick tired and Manson unamused, they tied up and that ended the fight. Moose Jaw could beat us on the score sheet but we wouldn't go down without a fight, not even in those last two seconds of the game. That was the kind of leader Rick Rypien was. He brought David and Goliath to life.

Everybody knew it for the next week. Rick could barely see out of that eye. His cheek touched his visor, so he took it off in practice. Every time he came down on me, I knew I was facing somebody who would be a winner.

Rick signed a pro contract at the end of that season and battled his way into the NHL a couple of years later.

Becoming a Leader

I'm not the first guy to write about leadership. There are libraries full of books on this subject and that highlights its importance. You already know that as a winner you need to understand your purpose. Men who've already won also know that chasing your purpose can't be done alone. As humans, we are social creatures. We form alliances. We use emotion to inspire. Through these two things, we can step up and bring others on board with our purpose, taking everybody to a higher level.

Hockey has many shining examples of leaders who step up with teammates who follow. Mark Messier is often cited as one of the greatest captains of all-time. In the 1994 NHL playoffs, he guaranteed that his New York Rangers would beat the New Jersey Devils when facing elimination. This guarantee made front-page news in New York. It was a ballsy move. Messier stepped up the next game and potted a hat trick. The momentum of the series totally shifted and the Rangers eliminated the Devils.

Now for you to be an effective leader, you don't have to make guarantees. However, you do have to put your money where your mouth is. Of all the great captains and leaders I played under, most had one trait in common—they'd step up and do the dirty work when everybody else wouldn't. The story of Rick Rypien is one of the first shining examples I saw of this. Even though we had given up the game, Rick wouldn't go down without a fight, one he was almost assured of losing. Rick was willing to take the blows in order to show that our team wasn't allowed to back down. Every day when I'd see that black bruise under his eye, I simply couldn't let up. It was a constant reminder, and that inspiration didn't need to be the rah-rah sort.

Whether it is in business, family, or hockey, inspiring others can be done in a few ways. The first form, often hard for men, is to actually express what you find compelling about your purpose. My online education hub for hockey parents, the Junior Hockey Truth, is guided by a mission: to help bantam and midget players (and their parents) succeed at their dream of playing junior hockey. Every piece of media I create or produce runs through that mantra. To my amazement, once this started being my focus, other hockey people started messaging me in support of my site. The more this happened, the more I started telling my story of *why* I thought the site was important—my parents didn't have a guide for how to navigate the waters of junior hockey, so I created one. I want to help those parents. People can get on board with that mission and that purpose. It's not that people love me personally; they love what I'm trying to put back into the world (or so I hope), and that is why I'm contacted for speaking engagements and coaching inquiries.

The key turning point for me in my mission is that I'm not afraid to be vulnerable about it, to risk myself. Throughout this book, for example, I relay a lot of personal stories, and many of them feature my mistakes. Much of the content on my website is created from mistakes as well. Few people laugh. If anything, parents are thankful I highlight these same mistakes so their sons know not to make them. This information gets passed around and my site grows. By showing that vulnerability, I gain credibility. I've been through the pain so their sons don't have to go through it.

When you're trying to achieve a purpose, you need to let people know why you're chasing it and to not stifle yourself while doing it. Let people know what drives you. Show them you won and expose your failures for what they are. As long as you can show you're accountable for your losses they can actually work in your favor. Losses show you've been through some battles.

As a leader, you need to be the one leading the charge toward your purpose. When you're on the clock you have to be on your purpose. Your dedication and passion toward your goal will inspire others to help you.

Exercise

When you want to inspire others toward a cause, you can dig deep as a leader to get them on board by:

1. Identifying the *why* of task, your purpose. Why is the task or your major purpose so important? People need to know this.

2. Using emotional pull. Clearly express what the purpose means to you. When others understand your struggle and journey, they are more likely to help you. Develop your story and tell it.

3. Walking the walk. True leaders lead from the front. Act in alignment with your purpose. Even if you're leading a group and not doing the grunt work, you still need to show that your role takes on a share of the burden (even if that role is delegation and management.)

4. Showing others how their contribution is valuable. Show verbal appreciation, help others with their purpose and forge relationships. People only want to give value when they receive value in return. Make sure to give as you get.

Chapter 9
WINNERS VALUE THEIR TIME

One by one, they turned the corner into the dressing room behind our bench, tossed their sticks at our trainer, Leo, and perched their asses on the edge of their stalls. The boys didn't slouch because they knew better. That would have earned a verbal lashing. They knew to sit up straight after a loss.

I was always the first one in the room. Every game. I stood at the end of the bench, swinging open the door, hair slicked back. As the backup, I didn't play. I just took up space. I was the first one in the room because otherwise I was in the way of the exit. You didn't want to get in the way after a loss.

"You guys have wasted my time for the last time," Tom, our coach, said emerging from his office into the dressing room. "All week, we practice, over and over to prepare to play these guys, and you don't show up.

"Evan, how many times did we say don't clear the zone on your backhand?"

"A lot."

"Yes. Fuckin' rights, a lot. They've been telling you that since you were in novice and you still can't do it," Tom said.

Evan, the young rookie, had already learned it was best to let the coach hear what he wanted to hear in these situations. Being honest made it worse. We all knew the honest answers. So did the coach. Being honest meant we knew our mistakes, that we knew better. Keeping quiet, that omission, let the coach reinforce what we all knew: our error in losing. If he didn't get control of the ship in the aftermath of a stormy loss, he'd sacrifice those starting the silent mutiny. It was all about control.

Tom shoved his hands in pockets and looked down at his feet as he shuffled across the room. He became hushed.

"Guys, do you think I like staying up until 3 a.m. watching video of us making the same mistakes over and over? I don't want that, guys. I don't want to yell at you. I don't want to sit you out and I don't want to skate you. I really don't want that."

He stopped and turned toward the row of veterans.

"Merce, do you want that? Louie, you don't want that, do you? Muff, I know you don't want that."

Tom could get you to hang off his words in his own particular way. He had this way of pacing his speech to match his mood. When he was mad he'd slow down and draw you in, and you'd just be hanging on— waiting for it—for the yell to come at you.

"So this is what I can't understand. Why the—" Tom pulled his hand from his pocket and pointed it toward the door, "Why the fuck do you guys do this to yourself every second game? Put your hand up if you thought you played a full sixty minutes tonight. Put 'em up. I want to see them."

Three players raised their hands.

"Yes, Muff, you did…Carter, put your hand up…Chewy, you played a full sixty?"

Chwedoruk was a veteran and a smart-ass. He was talented, he was drafted, and he was never going to realize his full potential. He was too immature. I didn't know why, but I always felt he wouldn't make it all the way.

"I played their top line all night and was plus one."

"Weren't you on the ice for their winning goal, when you were caught in their end pinching? Because you know we don't pinch in the last ten minutes, don't you Chewy? Or were you thinking about that hot tub you were in before the game?"

"That was to warm up my groin," Chewy said.

"To warm up your groin, eh?," Tom said.

"Yeah, Leo said to warm it up. That's what I did it before every game when I was in Dallas."

"And are you in Dallas?"

"No, but—"

"Are you in Dallas right now? Is there a big green star right here?" Tom said, pointing circles at our red carpet.

"No."

"And does that hot tub stop you from pinching in their zone in the last ten minutes?"

"No, but—"

"No. That's what I thought."

After a game, win or lose, Tom was the first one off the bench after me. When we won, he would stick in the room and watch us high-five one another over our little victory song on the stereo. When we lost, he'd make us sit and stew in silence. He'd stamp into his office, look over the game sheet for a second and do a quick rally with the assistant. He'd then enter the room with a plan, one of a speech that reinforced the moral of losing. A loss can never be taken lightly. Once one loss is a joke, all losses are a joke. We liked to joke around in the room. It was our second home. Coaches only like to joke when you win.

"I'm trying to talk here and you're arguing with me," Tom said. "Dallas? Fuck me. I don't think you're going to be pinching like that in Dallas. You can be damn sure of that.

"Listen here," Tom said, and turned around. "We practiced all week to prepare for this game and we fucked the dog. I'm sick of doing breakouts, and I'm sick of bag skating you guys. I don't know if you are sick of listening to me or you just don't care, but I care. I care. I care about my time because I am not going to come here every day with a plan and have you lie to me and not execute it. Tomorrow morning at 5 a.m., I want you to be here. We will be on the ice at 5:30. You guys can't focus enough to remember what to do at any other time, so we're going to skate first thing in the morning, when nothing else is going on. You'll have nothing to distract you, and this better be your best practice of the year. There isn't much of a year left, and we can't keep playing like we have."

Tom wrote a big "5:30 a.m." on the board and walked across the room past Chewy.

"Five-thirty, don't waste my time....And Leo, drain that fucking hot tub."

——— ——— ———

The next morning I sat up with a pounding head. The agonizing screech of the alarm clock on my ears screamed only louder on less than four hours of sleep. I downed my breakfast, a Gatorade, and drove through the darkness to the rink.

Colin, the Zamboni driver, greeted me at the door. He slept in the player's lounge overnight. It was just easier than going home. He was the only jovial man that morning.

The boys rolled into the room by the carload. Mark and Terry and Liam, Johnsy and Merce, and all the rest. The first ones scavenged through the leftover bagels and orange slices Leo left out for us from the game. I went for my usual pre-practice run—I needed to be focused this morning. In a situation so tense, you never want to be the one who doesn't rise up. I knew this practice was a ruse, a puffing of the coach's feathers, but I still snapped my heels together and played my role. I wanted to win as bad as anybody else, and we trusted the coach. We had to trust him. He decided who played.

Carter rolled in last.

"Merce buddy, why don't you turn that stereo on so we can get pumped up for this hell bagger," he said.

The music played, the boys got dressed and we hit the ice at 5:29. There wasn't a puck in sight. A puck, at this practice, that would be a joke. We knew what was coming. We knew it was a bag skate. If your brain doesn't work in a game, your lungs will work in practice. That was the old school maxim of coaching. Tom stepped on the ice.

"Leo, go get the pucks," he said as we all skated over to him. He didn't even have to blow the whistle. We were on our toes this morning.

"Listen. I could skate you guys into the ground, but that's going to do nothing to prepare us for this weekend. I want a crisp, short practice today. I want every pass on the tape. This better be your best practice of the year. I know you will deliver. Line up in the corners."

I was as surprised as anybody in that kneeling gaggle of scared soldiers. We just received orders that we wouldn't be bagged. (A very good thing.) The catch was that we were expected to be perfect. (A seeming impossibility.)

One by one the boys came down the walls and shot crisp ones into my pads to warmup. We stretched and did two-on-ones, then three-on-twos, then breakouts. It was simple stuff and we were flawless. Passes weren't missed. The boys had hustle. I dove and scrambled for every rebound. The clock clicked to 6:30 and we were off. It was short; it was sweet; it was flawless.

Tom walked through the room on his way out of the rink. It was an exit quicker than normal. His parting words were tied in to his speech from the night before.

"Men. That is how you practice. That is how you value your time. You did the work of two practices in one. We'll see you this afternoon and we'll do it again."

I knew to use my time in between for sleep.

Valuing Your Time

At his birth, a man is a millionaire. He has a wealth of time left to chase his purpose. On his death bed, that man is broke. Time is something he can never earn back.

No matter your age, wealth or background, you are not getting any younger. In fact, as your read this, you are actually using up your most finite resource—time. No matter how many achievements you accumulate or experiences you have, time cannot be replaced. Men who win know this. There are only so many ticks left on the clock before the horn blows on the game of life.

Often, young men think their happiness will be increased by earning more money so they can more stuff. I used to believe this too until I started thinking in terms of time. As the old saying goes, "Money doesn't make you happier, it just makes you more of who you already are." Buying stuff is only a temporary serotonin hit, and you can't buy durable happiness. Money can, however, make life a heck of a lot easier, and that frees up your time.

Wealth is evidence of success and can grant you time to chase more success. It allows you to delegate tasks in business; lets you pay more for the direct flight instead of the milk run with three layovers; etc. The problem occurs when men focus their time so intensely on wealth building that they lose focus of their core purpose—the reason that they started chasing wealth.

If you're a man who wants to put up wins, make your first focus on creating more time…more freedom. Freedom is winning for men. Don't lose direction by focusing on money first without an end goal, a purpose in mind. Make money to buy more freedom, not just to buy stuff.

My simple process for achieving this focus is to examine my situations for their strain on my time. Whenever I am faced with an obstacle—whether it is a daily nuisance or an overarching roadblock of my purpose—I try to find the solution to it that requires the least time. I'll often give up a bit of money to buy some time, rather than give up time to earn more money. Focus on time first.

For example, as I write this I've chosen to live in Austin, Texas for the winter. Flying direct almost anywhere is tough since one of the biggest airports in the world is down the road in Dallas. Flights almost always get re-routed through there. However, often I can find ways around this by paying extra to book a direct flight to New York or Los Angeles. I'll gladly pay an extra $100 to save three hours for a couple of reasons. First, since I do value my money and the time it took to earn it, I'm motivated to get $100 worth of value out of myself in those extra hours. Secondly, I can use those extra hours toward my purpose of growing my business to serve more hockey players. The more players I can serve, the more money I make *in time*. I'll make that $100 back times ten through leverage. (Always take leverage over security.) I'm paying now to make money later by valuing my time. Third, it's just nicer to say, "Nick, just make it easy on yourself—the hassle to save $100 is just not worth it." It's nice to value yourself like that and it sends a subconscious message of self-worth.

In this chapter's story, Tom used this principle on our team. Every day in practice we would practice breaking out of our zone only to falter in games. Tom had no problem going over something as simple as breakouts if that was what was required. What he had a problem with was going over breakouts and us not applying the practice. The time was not valued because we didn't apply the use of it to our purpose as a team. Vividly, I remember that 5:30 a.m. practice we had. It was our best practice of the year (and we won our next game.) Our focus was so sharp. It really felt like we packed two practices worth of work into one because we didn't let a moment get wasted. I still believe that the fact every one of us would rather have been sleeping forced us to realize how important being there was. We put the team's time ahead of ours for the purpose of winning. We had no choice but to give our time over to an early practice and that forced us to value it.

As a man, you need to figure out what your time is worth to you. The most successful entrepreneurs I know and CEOs I've studied all work out at some point during the day. They give up that hour of time because they know they'll get it back two-fold later. It's valuable for them to get up. These same guys also aren't afraid to pay for hotels near their meeting locations so they can save time getting to the meeting, rather than saving money staying somewhere cheaper while wasting more time driving.

Valuing time is one of my favorite principles because it forces you to realign your values. However, you're also required to make a major mental shift when doing this. You have to stop chasing what you think is important and step up and say that you are important, that your time is. You learn to value yourself and in turn, this draws more opportunity your way. You search for these opportunities where others won't because you don't have time to sit and wait for it.

Furthermore, you'll start setting boundaries on your time. A classic example of this was Tom telling us that if we were going to waste the team's practice time then he wouldn't allow us to do so—he stole our sleeping time to teach us a lesson. We hated that and it made a lasting impression. We learned the value of time through that lesson, and we had a much smoother practice and our mentality was forced to shift. Ask yourself how you command people to respect your time. Do they come prepared to presentations they make to your firm? Does your professor actually teach you something useful in class or are you sitting thirty wasteful hours each semester to earn a piece of paper? Where would your time be better spent in those moments? Finding the answer to that question will lead to more abundance and a greater focus on your purpose. It's a step toward more wins.

Exercise

In order to increase your time, you need to take inventory of how you're using it before you can realign your focus. Use this process to create more time:

1. Chart out your typical day from the time you wake up until the time you go to sleep. Mark off tasks that are taking you too long or that you don't enjoy doing.

2. Mark which of these tasks you can delegate. Think outside the box. For example, have you considered using a laundry service instead of doing your laundry? Do you listen to audio books at the gym or in your car while commuting?

3. Of the tasks that cannot be delegated, can you change the system you use to do them in order to compress them into less time?

4. Take your biggest task of the day and do it as your first. You will have the most energy at the beginning of the day. Your time will be used most efficiently on what is most important.

5. Last, identify what you will do with your newfound free time. Will the extra time to relax in the evenings improve your family life? Can you hit the gym more often now? If you're spending money to delegate tasks, will your new free time allow you to enter more money earning activities? Identify your new activity so you can be steered toward it.

Chapter 10
WINNERS USE DELIBERATE PRACTICE

He's daaddd. Let's sploosh him down the toilet," Marek said, his nose pressed to the glass of the fish tank. He made a scooping motion with his hand. "Git the...you know, like spoon."

Marek was Czech. It was his second year in North America, and sometimes it sounded like his second day speaking English. He was a couple years older than me and drafted to the NHL. While I practiced stopping pucks that year as a rookie, Marek practiced putting them in as a veteran. It was always a challenge when Marek came down on me; his hands spun viscous dekes and dangles faster than I could track them.

I passed him the like-spoon fish net and he ran it through the water, careful to only catch the one dead fish.

"It's called flush, not sploosh. You flush the toilet," I said.

"Flush? It like poker, ya?"

"Kinda of. Same word."

"We just tell billet, 'He daaddd and have to go.' They're not get mad. He just die." Marek held the net and we both proceeded to the bathroom. He enjoyed caring for the goldfish in our basement, even naming them, and didn't want to throw this one away. On the ice, he could be a hothead sometimes. Marek would chop on your ankle on the backcheck to get even with you, but if you were on the same team you were his buddy. He could be the gentlest guy you meet in the right situation.

After hearing the toilet suck and gurgle, seeing the fish swirl round we went back to our primary task, finding something to watch on TV. Marek grabbed the remote from beside the tank and flipped through channels on the big screen.

I always found the Europeans, the "Euros," interesting. What they valued on and off the ice was different than most North Americans. And to top it all, you couldn't lump them all together. The Swedes and Finns worked their asses off, for instance. The Czechs and Slovaks, in my experience, were different. Most wouldn't have minded to play in the Show, but they took the casual approach to it. They could work hard, but only when they wanted to. Many were just happy to go home and play pro. It really depended on the individual.

Marek wouldn't have minded either route, but that didn't stop him from staying up late and watching Trailer Park Boys with me. "Who he is? He have eyes like fish," Marek would ask and laugh. "He's best." He was referring to Bubbles, the Canadian googly-eyed hero, the character who rivaled Don Cherry in popularity at the time. Sometimes Marek would stay up until 3 a.m. just watching him.

The pet fish and mockumentary comedy were amusing, but what really amazed me about Marek was how he could stay up until 3 a.m. and still be ready for practice the next day. He would get up at noon, eat, and I'd come home from school and we'd drive to the rink together. Truthfully, Marek hated the practices. He hated going over systems. He hated backchecking. He hated getting dirty in the corner. However, Marek loved working on his stickhandling for an hour after practice if he had the time. While most guys would use that time to shoot around, or maybe take five minutes to do a little haphazard drill, Marek was specific.

Back home in "Czech" as they all called it, young players didn't focus on games so much as skill building. They stared with individual skill building. Where North American players focused on being game-ready and learning through trial by fire, the Euros set deliberate drills in practice and played half the games North Americans did. Marek liked playing more games in North America, but he was always surprised how we practiced so little in-between them. He wondered how we could improve on our mistakes when we played more than we practiced. It was a different mentality.

So while everybody fooled around for fifteen minutes after practice, playing competitive games or doing a fun shootout, Marek stationed himself in front of the penalty box. He'd line up ten pucks with a foot between each. From the bench, he'd grab an eight-inch piece of ABS plastic pipe and slide it over the shaft of his stick. For the next fifteen minutes, he'd go in and out of the pucks, forward and back. He'd bounce the puck off the boards, catch it and go through again. Then he'd do it all in reverse, then with one hand. He'd do this over and over and over until the Zamboni was coming out. While the rest of the team was getting ready to ride the bikes or shower up before a team meeting, Marek would be honing skills. He was always the last one to leave…I was his driver.

There was nobody I played with who had hands quite like Marek. I played with many skilled players, even future NHLers, but this guy had it down. That's probably why he is playing pro in Europe still to this day.

I have no doubt that much of it had to do with that line of pucks and piece of pipe he gripped. The man valued stick handling and he worked on it consistently. Not only that, be he was also methodical in his approach. He didn't just dangle around the ice. He didn't just practice breakaways. He grinded it out after practice in a monotonous drill that forced him to focus and push his abilities. That deliberate practice made him the best stick handler I ever played with.

Practicing With Deliberation

Deliberate practice is a concept receiving increased study today in academic circles. Most people now know it as fact that you need to practice ten thousand hours at a skill in order to master a skill, but few cite what should go into that practice. I first came across this concept years ago reading a quotation from Eric Lindros in some kids hockey book. "It's not the amount of time you spend at practice that counts; it's what you put into that practice." I wish that at the time I'd known he was referring to deliberate practice.

Deliberate practice put another way can be called practicing with a purpose. It's working on a skill with a high level of intensity and specificity. The difference between just practicing for the sake of practice and deliberate practice lies in your focus. An elite hockey player, for example, will line up one hundred pucks at the top of the circle and aim to go bar-down each time with full-force. However, if he just goes out for a wheel and fires pucks at an empty net all afternoon, that is not deliberate practice. The latter may actually spend more time on the ice, but he won't be squeezing as much skill-building juice out of that time.

The hardest part about deliberate practice is that it isn't always fun to kick off. There are often more fun alternatives. If you want to work on your stick handling, you can grab a goalie and play breakaway games for a half-hour after practice. You'll get value from it too. However, it doesn't compare to grinding it out with boring, often rudimentary drills that force you to move the needle one percent further. You have to pass the modern standard of instant gratification if you want improvement in a specific area. You need to put in the time.

Today's society has evolved. We no longer maintain the standards of apprenticeship in one craft like in centuries past, except in the most manual of trades. Nowadays, many men make the mistake of working to earn money for themselves or somebody else when they start out instead of working to build a bevy of skills. They work to earn, not to learn. Admittedly, I'm a results guy. I want my labor to pay off. It's part of what I think of as "working smart." However, men in the first half of their life need to also think long-term. In order to build something great, men need great skills or the experience to find another person who can apply those skills.

I once had a mentor, Boris, who co-founded a very successful company I won't name but you may have heard of. He told me the story of working on his fashion for years. Boris was anything but a pretty boy. He cast an impression of one heck of a powerful man in the suits he wore. In need of a suit myself, I thought I would tap into Boris' mastery and ask him for the latest trends in men's fashion.

"I don't follow trends," he said. "I use timeless fashion."

"Timeless fashion?" "Yes. Most guys think that fashion is about what's hot and trendy, and that is why most guys dress bad. They don't realize what colors work with their skin tone or what tailoring and cut flatters their body type. I don't look to trends. I say, 'I want a checkered shirt' and I go get one made one that will fit and flatter me. I don't care what people call trendy. It won't be trendy next year, but what I get will always look good."

Obviously, given my lack of knowledge, I was anything but a guy who put thought into fashion. If it fit and didn't raise alarms, that worked for me. Boris changed that. After talking to him more, Boris, a venture capitalist, told me that every time he travelled to places like London for meetings, he'd stop in at Savile Row and talk with tailors. He studied timeless dressers like Fred Astaire. For him, developing one of the most powerful images I ever saw on a man didn't come from buying what he saw in advertisements. It came from studying the art of fashion. Buying a shirt wasn't means of putting clothes on his back; it was an extension of his masculinity.

At the end of our conversation, I asked Boris why and how he had learned so much about a topic most guys don't put much thought into.

"In the nineteen twenties and thirties, every man knew his suit. Part of being a man was being able to present yourself. When I started having success with my company, I looked to those men who were more successful than me, and I noticed everything they did was on purpose. Even the way they dressed was on purpose. So I started studying all of the best dressers the same way I studied business, and that's when I started to notice the littlest things that make a big difference.

"You can dress like this," he said, pointing at his chest, "but it took me twenty years of studying. You can't just do it overnight."

Even as a totally clueless dresser at the time, I had total respect for what Boris said. I got it. In the same way, that I could marvel over how a centerman would grip his stick before a faceoff, Boris applied that same level of study to how he chose cufflinks. The more I followed this concept of deliberate practice, the more I saw it everywhere.

The hardest part you'll find about instituting deliberate practice—you've probably done it before, you just may not have realized it—is that it requires effort. That work takes mental capital and sometimes it takes the fun out of the process. You have undergo toil in the process to get the desired result. You must be in the moment and focus on the skill you are developing. If it helps, know that it will pay off for the greater good down the road.

Any man who wishes to improve the necessary skills needed to chase his purpose must use deliberate practice. This specific type of skill building through repetition works on the ice, but also in business and hobbies. Winners know that they need to focus harder than the casual player. They focus on what they need, develop or find a system they can use to improve their specific skill, and then they hone it and hone it until they break through to a new realm.

Exercise

Figuring out a system for deliberate practice of your skill is not difficult. What can be challenging is finding one specific skill to work on when you have many things you wish to accomplish. With deliberate practice, you want to focus on only a few skills at a time, perhaps even one per area. Here's how:

1. Every man has his core purpose, and within it are different avenues of skill needed to move toward that purpose. Pick one avenue. For example, if you wish to master the guitar, pick one style to practice.

2. With your avenue chosen, create a plan that encompasses time and specificity toward your skill. For our guitar example, you may want to put in an hour every day toward learning one song that is considered a staple in your genre of music.

3. You may not know the answer on day one, but at some point you will reach a high degree of certainty at your skill. When you reach that point, you must throw new twists into the skill. For our guitar example, learn to play the song at different speeds or in a different style.

4. Once you can work your skill inside and out and you have thrown in twists, find what the next step up the ladder is with your skill. For guitar, learn a more difficult song and pick one

that challenges you. The purpose of deliberate practice is to hit a "flow" state, where you are constantly challenged enough that you are kept interested, yet it is not so difficult that the task is impossible to work on. Take pride in the challenge of the process.

Chapter 11

WINNERS KNOW
WHEN TO RESET

I had had larger steaks back on the ranch than the one sizzling on my plate. We all had one.

"Do you think we're going to stop on the way home?" I said to Creighton. We all sat segregated at a booth full of rookies.

"We better. It's a four-hour drive," Carlson said, butting in from across the table. Tony, the fourth participant, said nothing. He never said anything.

All four of us were rookies on the Regina Pats. All four of us wouldn't last two years on the team.

Our trainer was Saltzy, a burly man with beard and tracksuit. If you spent a minute with him he could make you laugh and it didn't matter who you were. A trainer has an interesting place in the dressing room. While he has a bond of friendship with the older players, he's the only guy who is not a rookie who talks to the rookies. He must also maintain an air of respect as a member of the staff. Everybody wants something from the trainer and he has a budget on time, money and sanity. If the coach changes lines an hour before practice, the trainer has to get out a whole new set of practice jerseys. If a player needs laces or to get his skates sharpened, he has to go to the trainer. At lower levels of junior, if the trainer handles equipment *and* injuries he doesn't have time to mess with jerseys and tape because he's already taping up an ankle or a wrist. Trainers get close to everybody on the team, but everybody wants something from them. When needed, the trainer instantly commands respect. He is the baker operating the bread line as everybody lines up outside his little dressing room workshop. You snap into line when he tells you.

"Is there something fuckin' funny about losing?" Saltzy said. He locked eyes with me, then with Creighton. You would have needed a steak knife to cut the silence he left hanging in the air.

"No," Creighton said. I sat stunned.

"Is there something funny about losing, back up?"

"No."

"Good. Then eat your steak," Saltzy said. "There is nothing funny about losing."

Saltzy was right. By this point in the season, we'd lost enough. Getting knocked off our purpose, not following the systems, not being accountable to each other—we'd really done it all that year to fill the 'L' column. And frankly, we were sick of it. Nobody liked losing. That's why it stung so much when the coaches would rally us for a, as one coach was fond of calling them, come-to-Jesus meeting. These were the meetings that happened late at night after a road trip, or on the one day off you were supposed to have each week. They were never rushed and were laced with deep analysis and introspection. Nobody was yelling. It was more full of pleading. In the movies, a come-to-Jesus meeting would have ended with everybody rah-rahing and gathering at the center of the room for a group high-five. It would end with a cutaway of the defining game where the team's season would turn around as they went on to victory. Sadly, they just don't end like that in real life.

Everybody leaves a come-to-Jesus meeting cautiously optimistic at best. They should happen only once a year, but when your team has them once a month starting in November, you start to assume Jesus isn't coming. Our gatherings ended anti-climatically—no high-fives, no rah-rahs—with a weight of responsibility on our shoulders and the reality of mounting losses tethered to us.

We would have had a meeting that Friday night, but we had bigger problems to contend with outside. There was a road-blocking snowstorm. Our four-hour jaunt home from Brandon to Regina would turn into a seven-hour sojourn. Worse, Brandon was in our division. This meant that we would have to play again the very next night at home. There was no mandated break between divisional games. I just tried to sleep through it.

We knew the night would be filled with tosses and turns and brakes from the bus. Some guys chose to bring ratty old blankets and sleep on the floor. In winter, the floor is soup on tiles from all of the melted snow on your dress shoes. No matter where you lay, you can't pass out for anything resembling sleep. The bus ride after a loss is no joy ride. We rolled into Regina at 4 a.m., just enough time to wake up for school at seven.

The next night we were exhausted. Beat. Nothing extra to give in the game, which was a loss to Moose Jaw. This was our last game before the big home stretch toward the playoffs. Come-to-Jesus meetings happen this time of year too. When I saw the manager walk into the room, I thought this one would be big.

Managers rarely join meetings. The only time they come down is to announce a tectonic trade. The room gets a certain silence when they step in.

"Gentleman," he said. "Sit down."

Our manager was kind of a gruff speaker. Businesslike, professional, no-nonsense. Everybody sensed this. The vets seemed a little more at ease than us rookies as he spoke.

"I heard you've been planning a party...You guys have been playing a lot lately. We need you ready for the homestretch."

I was at school that day, so I didn't know there would be a party. I didn't think we'd ever be allowed to go out past 10 p.m. that season given how poorly we'd played. Knowing that other guys took the time to plan one was almost like a cruel joke for me. I didn't know such bonding retreats were possible.

"I know where you're going tonight. Go out, have your party, but nobody drives. Understand me? Bring in your cab receipts and be ready to work Monday."

The coaches crossed the dressing room floor, following the manager to their office. We sat in our soaking gear and looked at each other. Not a peep. We were stunned at the free rein of opportunity thrown at us.

"Are you ready to party, boys?" Shelly said, and so the night began.

I don't recall much else of that night, and I didn't do anything significant enough the next day to remember it. However, I do know that when we came in Monday there was a different energy in the room. Voices were piping, chirps were flying, the ice seemed a little more crisp and the shots were zinging off the bar. We had some jump back in our step and we were ready to battle for our final playoff spot. The spring was back in our stride. We were reset for the stretch drive.

Pressing Reset

As men, we get caught in ruts. Our focus becomes our work, our purpose. One of masculinity's greatest strengths and weaknesses is its connection to external events and meaning. For the masculine, the journey through an experience is less important than what the outcome of that experience is. Thus, as men we tend to be outwardly driven, seeking signposts of success on the way to achieving our goals, our purposes.

While this mechanism is a good thing when we are seeking results, it can also lock us in to a very narrow focus. If you've ever met a man who knows nothing but work, you've met a man who lacks what many self-proclaimed self-help "gurus" call "balance" in his life. I've been one of these men more often than I'd like to admit, so I know how this feels.

It's not just a matter of men needing more "balance" in life. I believe being in perfect balance all the time leads to mediocrity. You give equal weight to things of importance and unimportance alike. What may serve of greater importance is having a reset button.

A reset button, metaphorically speaking, is a short time of release from purpose. It works when a man is so tied into his purpose, so filled with pressure, pushed so deep that he can't shake out of his thinking. His consciousness is locked into one realm, his nervous system protected by his ego. This is when he needs a break. Men who are so entranced in their work need to devise a method or a time to release and be free of their tasks. They need to change the filter in their mind. This is not getting knocked off their purpose; it is recharging the energy.

In my story above, as so often happens during the playoff stretch, our team had an intense schedule. We were locked in deeply, playing three to four games each week. As players, all we would do is go to and from rink to rink. On a losing streak, the tension was mounting within the team. Players would start bickering and the staff would be pulling out their hair. Everybody was mentally exhausted without really being aware of it.

The conventional wisdom for refocusing a man (or a team) is to work hard, to give more effort than has been given before. It's almost as if the man needs to prove to himself that he truly dedicated to the task, like hard work owes him results. This is not true. In hockey terms, it leads to squeezing your stick as a means of getting out of a scoring slump. What a man really needs is to shift his focus, briefly. He needs time off.

In this chapter's story, with his team that was slumping, our manager recognized that if we kept playing under such duress we would either shut down totally or, being teenagers, end up having a party at a very disadvantageous point of the schedule. He sought to circumvent this and let us reset. We were set free for an evening. Many times in life this strategy can work for other men.

If you are working on big project for work or school, or if you are trying to grow your business, you're going to need to schedule time off. And during that time off you need to totally leave your core purpose behind. This means cell phone off, laptop put away, tools left in the truck. Winners know that they have to hit the reset button to draw in new energy. The time away from their purpose will benefit their purpose in the long run. The win in this situation is taking time off to replenish. When this is done, the winner can return back to his purpose with an even harder hitting vitality and clarity. It rejuvenates focus and motivation.

Exercise

Hitting the reset button should be easy. Making time for it is the hard part. Here's how to find the time:

1. Identify an activity you enjoy that requires your full attention and thought, does not relate to your purpose, and perhaps has a physical element to it. A good example is lifting weights or running, or playing with your kids.

2. Identity at what point in your day or week you can do this activity where it will enhance your ability to chase your purpose, i.e. where it will have a restorative effect on you.

3. Plot time into your schedule to undertake this activity. Remember, the goal is for you to reset and ultimately boost your energy, not to be distracted.

Chapter 12
WINNERS HAVE IDENTITY

I really shouldn't write about my time with the Surrey Eagles. While I was there, those short two months, the players defied every principle I've stated in this book. Yet, without question, they were the most dominant team I ever played for.

Surrey was a party. Our motto was literally, PH^2. Play hard, party hard. On many teams, breaking curfew was sin. In Surrey, it was the veterans' suggestion. On other teams, being accountable defensively was a requisite. In Surrey, we'd just score another goal when we broke down. We were a tier II level team, aka Junior A, filled with tier I castaways like me. The players who weren't cuts from leagues above were NHL picks—high picks. With the exception of two or three teams in the BCHL, nobody could run with us. Many times there were more NHL scouts at our games than there were when I played at higher levels. We'd just show up and piss pure skill all over the ice until you'd think it would melt. It was rock 'n' roll, run-and-gun hockey every night.

In a way, Surrey was accountable. No matter how late the party went, the players still showed up the next game and often won. But more than anything, what made us good—even downright cocky— was the belief we had. The boys truly believed they were unstoppable. In practice, the forwards would dance down the wall and pick the top corner. Before games, everybody spoke with a tone of expectancy. They was no *try* in Surrey, only a belief that we would *do*. And at the parties after, somebody would raise the keg like it was the Stanley Cup.

This expectation came built in when you made the team. We were a "daddy ownership" club. These teams existed in other parts of the world, but not in B.C., except for us. In a daddy ownership situation, the owner is a player's father. He buys his son a place to play. This was the son's final season, the one to do the winning. I didn't complain. I wanted to win just as much as anybody else.

With such high expectations, you came into Surrey knowing that every stall in the room would only be filled with somebody who made the team better that day. There was no planning for the future. Everybody on the team thought winning it all was a given. The coaches, the trainers, the players, the fans—we all believed it.

We were as cocky as they came and we expected to win.

Glen Sather, manager of the Edmonton Oilers dynasty during the eighties, said that he didn't mind if his players were a little cocky. He liked that they walked with an expectant air when they came to the rink. When you come to the rink like that, and when you come prepared, you come with an expectation of winning.

That identity, one of an unshakable winner, was what made Surrey the B.C. champs that year. It is also what, I believe, made them fall immediately after, before they could win the national championship.

Halfway through the year I went back up to the WHL again. As a guy who had no NCAA eligibility, staying in Surrey didn't do me any good no matter how good the team was. I could only advance in hockey through playing in the WHL. When the coach called me into his office and said, "You did it," I took that chance and ran with it. Yet, I followed the team. I knew the personalities. You're always a little curious to see.

I saw the team win the league championship. They dominated on the way there, like I imagine they expected to do. Then they calved out at the national championship. They had competition finally. They got down in some games against other winners. Stating the facts, I knew they just couldn't win when the chips got down on them. They had too much ego. When you have identity *attached* to winning, an ego attached to the outcome, you can't deal with losing. You don't look at the losses. You can't mend your chinked armor. The team had all the cockiness and confidence needed to win, but there was no humble grounding to absorb a loss. Ego bit them when they needed to be humble.

The next year the team changed ownership. Many players on the team made it to the NCAA and the WHL and pro hockey. Some even had a small sip of coffee in the Show and continue to slug it out in the minors today. Others moved on to a regular life. The team is now back near the top in the BCHL with new owners, once again winning. In my short time there years earlier, I got a taste of it too.

Creating Identity

Winners see themselves as winners—nothing less. Nobody identifies themselves as a guy who ties. No winner would call himself a loser, even if he had been one in the past. The difference is that true winners know why they are winners. They know why they deserve to win and why they sometimes lose. This knowing comes through identity.

As a man, your identity is how you see yourself. When you close your eyes and think of all your capabilities, limitations, the things you'd do and the things you wouldn't dare, you are reflecting that self-image in your mind. The actions you take from this reflection are guided by it.

Look at the stats of lottery winners. They often lose their fortune within a year or two. They can't handle the money because their minds aren't prepared for it. Their capacity to hold is tied to their identity as non-millionaires. And even if they start calling themselves millionaires, they'll spend the money on the wrong things, the things millionaires don't, to lose everything they've won. Their self-image doesn't allow them the capacity needed to manage that money.

True winners have a sense of entitlement, an identity enabling their wins that comes from an internal source. They have lost enough that they don't fear losing anymore. They've found what not to do. Or, when they get on a winning streak and ride it, they know that they've been putting the requisite work into their wins so they value them more than somebody who is just handed a win. In my story above, in Surrey, the expectation was there to win (and admittedly, the team did win a damn lot), but when the chips got down, the team folded fast. They hadn't dealt with high pressure losses the way other teams had. The players felt entitled to win because they were told it was their year. Their winning identity was false; it wasn't core identity. I know this because I played on a team a few years later, Vernon, the winningest team in Canadian junior A history, who had the expectation of winning through discipline.

When you build an identity based on your entitlement through what you've earned, you have a core identity that cannot be shaken. You know *why* you feel like a winner and why you deserve to win. If you build your identity on false pretenses, you are just a prima donna. You have no backbone to your beliefs. Then when you do start winning, you'll attach ego to it. You don't understand the climb to the top of the hill when you drop yourself there. You're all outcome and no process.

True winners understand that their wins could turn to losses at any point. They don't count on it and don't bet on it, but they always keep their knees bent a little in case they need take off. The man who builds ego onto his identity will catch himself coasting. He walks with swagger because he thinks he has to, not because it's his own rhythm.

Hockey provides a great example of this. Any time a team is on a roll or has a great game, you'll always hear the interview after.

"What does this win mean for the team?"

"Well," the player will respond. "It's, ya know, good to get a big 'W' in their barn tonight. We know they're going to come out stronger next game, so we have to be prepared and take it one shift at a time. If we stick to our game we know we'll give ourselves a chance to win."

There is a winning identity in this example. It's evinced in the language. The player knows he can win, but he doesn't guarantee it. He doesn't berate the other team; in fact, he even qualifies that his team must only worry about themselves. There is no ego attached to the statement. Winners know that every day and night brings a new challenge. They focus on the process.

However, when a winner loses, you can also see the lack of ego in his language.

"It was a tough loss. We really didn't put in the right effort, so we came up a little short. We'll practice tomorrow and regroup and be ready for the next game."

You can also hear honesty in the words after a bad loss.

"We have to put this one behind us and pull together because we have some big games coming up."

You can tell in this example that the man doesn't carry ego with him. He doesn't blame the other team or the ref for his losses. He knows inside that he is a winner and that one battle does not make a war.

Winners keep the most even-keeled mind. They respect their purpose and know that there will be good days and bad days. They can't attach ego to their wins and identify with them. This will actually backfire.

If you identify yourself as a winner without having put in the work, or if you just appoint yourself one, you run the risk of having uncontrollable results. Your mood and your motivation will be determined largely by your results. If you win, you'll feel on top of the world. If you lose, you'll feel worthless. True winners don't let outcomes dictate their moods. Sure, they get mad after a loss and they can celebrate a win, but they don't dwell on these results. They shift their overarching focus back on the process and system that lead them toward their purpose. They squeeze the good that they can from their wins and the lessons that they can from their losses, and then they move on and add them to their process. Then they show up the next day. That's it. Their identity is that of a guy who has worked, who knows the system, who is smart enough to adapt, and most importantly, has the *capability* to win when he puts his system to work. They feel a certain destiny for winning through their process. It's tied to capability, not results. He can only tie identity to his *process* that leads to winning. He knows that he is a guy who can align everything as best he can and knows that it will never align perfectly. If the winner puts in the effort he is capable of putting in, he puts himself on the path to receive the desired result from the world. I truly believe that winners *command* respect, authority and results this way. The false winner, the one who ties ego and identity to his wins, he *demands* things from the world. He feels that past wins should bring him something in the future, regardless of the whether he continues the process or not. In a world where you are only as "good as your last game," you can't expect your track record to be your magnet for success. It's evidence, and it can be used to your mental advantage. Ultimately, you have to show up and put in the work. You have to trust in your process in the good times and in the bad. You need to build your mental foundation on your work through process so you can build a repertoire of abilities up. That is where you draw a winning identity from. If you demand that you be a winner and start tying identity to the wins, you'll fall flat in the face of small losses.

Exercise

A simple way to develop a winning identity is to define what you want to be, then have a mantra to go with its process. For instance, if you want to be a man who takes action in the face of adversity, even when you just don't feel like it, a good mantra can be, "I'm a man who takes right action over emotion, every time." This mantra says you're a man who does what he knows he should do, even if it may not feel pleasant to do it.

You make that mantra your default programming to guide you. Do this:

1. Define a single quality you want to add to your identity.
2. Create a mantra around that identity, starting it with "I am...."
3. Say this mantra every morning ten times when you wake up.

As a note, make sure the mantra revolves around an action you can take, not an end result. This will allow you to build identity but not attach ego to it.

Chapter 13
WINNERS HARNESS EMOTION

hree goalies sat together in a dimly lit dressing room beneath the stands. One was a first-round NHL pick, one was to be a first-round NHL pick, and the third was picking at the hole in the knee of his long underwear. I was the third one.

As each of us strapped on our pads, we all had our own thoughts, or at least I had mine. I thought about the shutout I got in exhibition, and about how I got pulled in the season opener. I also thought about how nice it would be to get a trade so I could play some games instead of being a backup. Given my age, nineteen, this was basically my last year to catch some NHL scout's eye. I finally felt confident playing in the WHL. I just needed a chance to get in some games. Being the oldest of the three goalies in that shadowy room, I knew I was the most likely to be traded. The market for nineteen year-old backups is always slim, but trades happen.

Bob popped his head into the room. He was our general manager, one of my favorites. He could be kind, he could be intense, but most of all he cared about his players. I respected Bob a lot and still do.

"Nick," he said. "I need you to come to my office."

No explanation of why. My mind raced.

Was I traded? Possibly. Was I sent down? That was a probability. Was it something totally random? Doubtful. You never got called down to the manager's office for that.

"Should I change?" I said, uncertain if my long underwear would be acceptable for an office trip down the hall.

"No, that's fine."

Our little room went silent. On a hockey team, good news is shared and celebrated, but bad news is delivered alone. It's business. Alone, nobody can gauge your reaction when you receive it.

I walked past the secretary and Bob welcomed me to his office and closed the door. I tried to crack a smile and sit at attention, bracing for the impact of what would come next.

"You're not going on the ice today," Bob said. "We're going to send you down…I've tried to trade you, and we'll keep trying, but nobody has room right now for goalies. You need to play and we need to play our guys."

That was the first time I was no longer part of that team. I was no longer one of *their* guys. Yet, I wasn't totally surprised. Bob and I talked. He was generous. I would still be part of the organization. I would be an emergency call up. I would get some more scholarship money. It was the best I could hope for from an inevitable situation. Too old at nineteen, I headed back to that dimly lit dressing room and packed up my bag.

I had thought about this possibility for weeks. When you're a fringe player, you always know that the axe can fall on your neck at any time.

You can see its shadow looming from over your shoulder. You think you can run away in a last panic, but the axe is always bigger than you. It's inescapable and always hovering over you. When that axe strikes, off with your head, you go down a level. You get cut. Your hopes get axed, as they say.

What you do from that point on is up to you. I wanted to stay at the highest level possible, but after over two years of major junior, I still wasn't playing games. I kept getting stuck behind great goalies and I couldn't build consistency. My effort was sincere, but my fate deserved its direction—I didn't put up the results when I was given my chances. That's why, when the initial shock wore off, my disappointment turned to excitement at getting sent down. I had a chance to actually play and put up the better results I knew I finally could. I was a veteran and could be an impact player.

The following morning, I stopped by the rink to pick up my gear and sign some paperwork. My next stop was Penticton, B.C., a seven-hour drive. I left early and arrived during the team practice that afternoon.

Penticton had an old barn of a rink. I loved playing in it. It was a beat up relic where the wooden rafters, aged, were turning to black. The stands were all wood, closed in planks, with no seats. The buzz from the lights echoed when it was empty. Being so damn old, the rink was tiny, from an era when regulations didn't exist. It must have been ten or twenty feet short of regulation size. For a six-foot-five guy like me, I'd look seven feet tall to the shooters. I was ready to play and this was the top team in the league, maybe the country, for the second tier.

There was one problem. Penticton didn't expect me to get cut from the WHL until I was twenty.

"You're not going on the ice today," their manager said, when I arrived. "Let's go to my office and talk."

He sat me in his bunker office under the stands to explain their situation. Penticton also didn't have room for me. They had a goalie already. I was sent down a year too early for their plans. As a player, you're always somebody's soldier. You can't win alone. You always fit into a battle plan. An organization, an owner, a manager, they put together an army and you're one of *their* soldiers. You must lose your *self* or they'll get rid of you. Individuals only count in their pre-set combination within the group. If the combination is out of sequence, they'll turn you loose.

I talked with the manager for twenty minutes. He said I'd be loaned to the Canmore Eagles in Alberta for the season. Dropped yesterday, loaned today. I now had two teams who wanted me enough to keep me around, yet were pimping me out for something in return. Penticton was a first-place team and Canmore was second-last. I was weary.

"You're going to play a lot, and we need you to be ready for next year," he told me. "We're going to be making our big run next year. You need a ton of games now so you're ready to be our guy. We're going for a national championship here, nothing less."

At least I was *their* guy this time.

The manager wasn't lying. I could see the pieces of a championship team coming together and I did need to play some games too. I accepted his decision. I didn't really have a choice, and in that moment my resentment grew just a twinge. It was the beginning of my personal anti-hero tale I didn't see but could start to feel. In the meantime, I hopped in my car and headed east to Alberta.

When I arrived in Canmore, I did play...a lot. I did become an all-star, and I did turn down three scholarship opportunities that were in the bag while there. I turned them down because playing in Penticton would get me glorious opportunities and give me a chance to be a winner. I played my ass off (quietly) waiting for the year to end in Canmore. And that summer, I worked as hard as I ever did, until August tenth, two weeks before training camp.

The Penticton manager called me that evening. He just got word the goalie from the year before would be returning again after giving up his scholarship. He was twenty. I was twenty. Two twenty-year old goalies almost never play together, and nobody in the triangle wanted it. Being that I still hadn't actually played for this team who owned me for two seasons, I became frustrated. Whether it was by owners or managers, I felt that my strings were being yanked. I had one year to nail down a scholarship and I was sick of being told where I'd have to go to get it. I was a guy who never whined or complained, and I started feeling like that was why I kept getting danced around. I hung up the phone and I got angry. I didn't want my strings pulled anymore.

Within a week, my rights were shipped to Powell River, an isolated hippie town you could only access by boat. At that point, their organization was perilous. They were a last place team who traded their leading scorer for a bus the season before. To recap the prior year: I had went from the top junior league in the world, to what I felt was the top junior A club in the country, to being a patsy on loan, to being shipped to a last place club in Powell River. I felt sucked under the waves. I had two weeks left before camp.

Any time I wasn't at my summer jobs over the next week, I lay on the couch. I had no energy. I hated hockey. I hated spending the whole summer training four hours per day, working two jobs as a teenager so I could afford a trainer and membership to a sport-specific private gym with NHLers. It was all for a team that sent me to the junk yard, I thought at the time.

As junior players, we spent our whole lives chasing the dream of getting to that level. By the time you're twenty, nearly three-quarters of your life has revolved around hockey. Sure, high school is thrown into the mix, but that's just there to keep you out of trouble when you can't be on the ice. You have no alternative universe to play in. You know nothing different. You get up and think hockey before you even think to take your morning piss. It's always on your mind. That's what makes it so great and so tough when you start reaching your goals, the contracts and playing rights and elements beyond your control start to control your destiny. You're like a pro without pay in many ways. You lose the grip on your own fate sometimes and you can't escape hockey to another reality. Your life exists within this hockey world. It's all you've even known…so you keep spinning with it.

I headed to Powell River's camp, deflated. It was the worst attitude. When you head to training camp, there should be excitement in you. Everybody gets a new start in training camp. It's a clean slate. Anything is possible for the team. Nobody in the league has lost and nobody has put up a point. If you want to be a winner, it all starts in camp. It should have been better, but my attitude in Powell River sucked. I was a weak leader. My heart wasn't in it. I was in my final year of junior and had been a foster kid of every team. I wanted a home, and I didn't want to end it all on a loser. I demanded a trade, *my* trade.

Two weeks later, I ended up in Vernon, which was the winningest junior A franchise in Canadian history. They were also Penticton's greatest rival. For the first time in months, I felt light when I stepped on the ice in Vernon. My pads felt like pillows, not bricks. I was told that we were expected to win, and I was specifically told to shape up.

Our manager, Troy, reasoned with me, "This team will only go as far as you take us. We have a championship team here, but we need a championship goalie. I know you have it in you, but dammit you've got to show it." He called me out as a man not a kid, put his faith in me and told me to rise to the occasion. I obliged.

We blasted through the first two rounds of playoffs. My coach from Canmore also gave a university coach a great reference about me. In turn, that coach gave me my scholarship. But more than anything, those playoffs' highlight for me was the third round, the one before we made the league finals. We played Penticton, my nemesis.

I arrived in their musty old rink the night of the game, thinking it was no different than any other game. I knew I had to focus on the process of what got me to that point. I couldn't get all emotional even though I wanted to. I didn't *hate* Penticton for what they did to me. I didn't *hate* them because they were a rival. I didn't *hate* them because they were our opponents that night. I made a choice not to hate them. I shifted my focus on to myself and what I could control. The outside didn't control me. However, I'd be lying if I said that thoughts didn't creep into my mind of what they did to me. I took ownership. I didn't act angry, but there was a fire inside of me. I chose to harness that anger instead of letting despair own me. These were the thoughts I had the night before that first game. I addressed them and I moved on to play.

Penticton's barn was tough to play in. Not only was their strategy built around that now-retired rink, but so was their team. When many effective junior A teams took skilled or smaller players, Penticton had a mix. They had roles for each line where other teams just rolled four mashed lines. Their top guys were very dangerous offensively, and their checkers were very dangerous physically. Yet, I knew their dump-and-chase-and-crush-you plays; I knew their backdoor power play. That harnessed anger gave me incredible focus. We matched them shot for shot, and came out of the first two games with a split. We never lost after that. The second last game of the series, I got a shutout. We met them again the next night and I got another shutout. Rarely did I put up shutouts in my career, but in that series I had two. That's how we finished them. Harnessing the emotion elevated me to the best I'd ever played.

Harnessing Emotion

Hockey players, fans and parents are interesting people. We are subsets that are all driven to compete and to win. As with any adrenaline packed event, we also have the tendency to lose control of emotion. That doesn't just mean a retaliatory slash or yelling at a ref. Emotions can range from being overzealous in victory to being depressed in the face of adversity. They can jut outward to anger or give in gently to gratitude. Most importantly, we truly do have the ability to choose how we feel and that choice becomes habitual very fast. Since all events and patterns are neurologically tied to emotion, when we choose our feeling it will crop up again and again. Our actions follow these feelings.

In-between the time when a stimulus occurs and our response happens is a space for choice. Our brains fire off pulses through our synapses that give us a gut reaction. After it fires that time, delay happens. Luckily, before we choose to act on that firing we can stop ourselves and choose a different way. Our human brains have this advantage over all other species. Interestingly, the more these synapses fire the easier it becomes for these gut reactions to happen. You have to be very careful in the responses you choose or they become automatic and harder to change. Gut reactions become hardwired.

Every time you face a loss (or in my story above, a trade) you have a myriad of reactions to choose from—anger, despair, hope, helplessness, etc. The reaction or emotion you choose in that moment can either propel you toward victory in the next battle or stifle you in your losing track. If I had chosen to just totally give up once Penticton traded me—and don't get me wrong, it's not like I smiled at it—the season would have been lost. I would have admitted defeat and I might as well have quit. But having no other option, I had to go play that fall, so I chose to play well. Initially, this wasn't easy; I did feel like quitting. You can only rack up so many losses before you start giving in to some doubt. However, by focusing on my process, embracing a kick in the ass from Troy after my trade, and keeping an even keel, I channeled those two years of uncertainty and anger into positive emotion.

All emotion has momentum. Just because you get angry at your boss or job, or because you get disappointed at a failed venture, it doesn't mean you can't move in the right direction. Anger can be a powerful feeling; it is an emotion that still allows for action. It keeps the ball in your brain rolling. You can use it to move on to the next step in turning around your purpose or honing your process. It's not a bad thing when used effectively. However, when you choose emotions of inaction, such as despair, you stifle yourself. You lose momentum because you wallow in the emotion. The reaction you take halts your action. It also makes it difficult for you to take a smart action when you're in a friction-filled emotional state. This is why I advise choosing anger over despair any day, as long as you use that anger to move you (not to hurt others, of course.)

At the same time, positive emotion is always best. It's the most fluid type of emotion you can choose. And as I say this, I'm not making a rah-rah, you-can-do-it, just-keep-positive speech. That kind of stuff doesn't work for the long-term. It's not a durable response. What you can do in the face of adversity is say, "Wait. What good can I pull from this?" or "I have to find the silver lining here," or at least, "Alright, well now it's time to start moving on." You want to choose a reaction that gives you positive momentum.

It's not always easy to do this. It's natural to receive bad news and to feel like swearing or to let your shoulders drop with a sigh of disappointment. It's where you pick yourself up and move from there that counts. During these dark moments, we often feel unappreciated or like all the work we've put in was wasted. Our *expectation* has let us down and we want to blame someone or have somebody make it better. We want answers. It's tribal. We want the strength of the tribe in times of adversity because that gives us security. Security is okay, venting is alright, but wallowing is death.

You can't wallow in times of adversity. You can use controlled anger if that at least starts moving you, or you can start searching for some good in the outcome, but ultimately, you have to look at the opportunity ahead. If you do this repeatedly, you'll automatically start looking for opportunity from adversity. You'll start mending your wounded ego on the path to reaching new success.

Successful men know how to harness emotion and use it all of the time. Patrick Roy got traded from Montreal in a fury and won the Stanley Cup multiple times with Colorado. Steve Jobs got fired from Apple and kept plugging away until they asked him to save the world's biggest company, which he turned it into by the time he died. Frat humor author Tucker Max had his first best-seller get rejected hundreds of times before it was published. He became a best-selling author. All of these stories come from taking events and molding them the right way.

So for the man out there reading this who has just been dumped, you have the perfect opportunity to find somebody better. For the entrepreneur whose tenth idea has failed, there will be an abundance of opportunities for bigger ideas around the corner. And for the player out there who has been cut from teams multiple times, it's an opportunity to find a team that values you so much that you get to be an impact player instead of a bench warmer. You just have to look for the opportunities in your defeat and find a way for it to motivate you, even if you get a little pissed off at first.

Exercise

If you've gone through a painful event lately and you're stuck in the rut of it, this is the process you can use to kick your ass out of it.

1. Identify the true cause of the event so you can make peace with the past. Did you get cut because you need to work on your skills more, or is it because there just wasn't enough room on the roster? Know the true reason as best you can.

2. Vow that although the negative feelings and reasons around the event exist, you're not going to give them your power. You're not going to let those feelings control you. You're in control.

3. Pick a "re-frame" for the event. Re-framing means that you're going to take the event, like a picture on the wall, out of its ugly frame and place it inside a shiny, positive one. Same event but presented differently. If you got cut, it becomes an opportunity to find a team that wants you. If you get laid off at work, it's your chance to find a better company.

4. Every time the negative emotion crops up, stop yourself and use your reframe. If you want to get mad at your old employer, stop and focus on the opportunity that lies ahead (And don't dwell if you have a hard time doing this at first, just keep moving forward in tiny steps.)

5. This is optional: Every time the negative emotion crops up, write it down. Answer back to it when you get home that night by writing down the re-frame. See yourself physically re-framing it on paper as you say it to yourself.

Chapter 14
WINNERS ARE PRESENT

It was almost as if I could feel the outer walls of my heart stiffen up as I put the phone down that spring evening. Still sixteen, I got the heaviest call of my life. The Portland Winterhawks had called to say they had dropped me. They no longer had me in their plans for the future. I had no training camp to attend that fall. The foundation I had built to get to the next level had cracked. Four months before the season, I had to start fresh.

When a player gets dropped by a team at sixteen or seventeen years old, he's in rough shape. Only through kicking some serious ass and having a bit of luck can he get picked up a second time. He's failed once and he has less time to make up for his mistakes before it's too late to make a junior team. I had few options, but I couldn't dwell on my misfortune. If I looked too far into the past trying to dissect the mistakes that led me to that moment, I would have gone into a tailspin. I had enough misfortune to deal with. I didn't need to analyze it. All I knew was that I wanted to play in the WHL and now I had to find a way.

Two weeks later I got off the school bus, opened the mail and pulled out a letter. This was the final letter I'd receive inviting me to a WHL training camp. It was from the Regina Pats. To put it in perspective, I pulled three letters out of the mailbox that spring inviting me to camps. The year before I had pulled out about fourteen.

My effort throughout the season was strong, but my results were not. I was already learning that the world demanded results, the winner's evidence. Effort wasn't enough. I now knew that I had to make something out of my few invites. That was what I had to deal with in the present. The past was done, the future couldn't be foreseen.

I waited another week, stopping at the mailbox every day on my way home from school, to see if more invites would come. None came. This was it, I thought. It scared me.

When you're an elite bantam or midget hockey player, your life revolves around hockey. You wake up and you think hockey, you go to bed with wet hair because you probably just got home from practice. If school wasn't mandatory, there would really be nothing else in your life. Hockey is your life. You *are* a hockey player. That's why getting only three letters was so disappointing.

In times of struggle or adversity, there is the great room for growth… but I didn't know that at the time. I'd learn this lesson later. At that time, I merely resigned myself to the fact that I would receive only those three letters, and that resignation is what allowed me to step forward. I knew what offers I had to work with, so I did just that—went to work.

I sat down one evening with my letters, Googled what each team's roster looked like and started making calls the next day. Two teams answered, but the call I remember most was with Regina.

"Hello…" I said nervously. "This is Nick Olynyk calling. I received your letter in the mail to come to training camp and I just wanted to ask you a few questions." "Sure," the voice on the other end said. It was the head scout of the Regina Pats.

"I see that both your goalies are coming back this year. I want to come to your camp, but I'm also wondering where I would fit in looking at your roster…I'm just trying to pick the best camp to attend."

I thought I was being picky. I didn't have the courage to make a stand for myself at that age. I was scared to sound weak. I was intimidated by somebody with a title. I was scared of what he would think. I just wanted to know if there was a chance. I was a lot of things, but mostly I was uncertain.

"Well, I'm not going to sit here and blow smoke up your ass," he said. "We have two goalies returning. One will be here. The other we're not too happy with. He's played okay, but he's kind of a liability with school and off ice. We want somebody to come in and push him. If you can push him enough, we'll give you a shot."

I was a little stunned. I'd talked to the man a whole thirty seconds and he said he wouldn't blow smoke up my ass. It was blunt. He said I had a shot and he said it with conviction. He really meant it. Rather than get too excited, I thanked him and filled out the training camp form. My little invite had moved a step forward on its own just by me acting on it in the present. I figured I'd give the WHL one last hurrah. Worst case scenario: I could grab some new, hard-to-find left-handed goal sticks in Regina while I was there.

Two sticks in hand that fall, I swung open the back door to the then Regina Agridome. As sometimes happens at camp, there was a goalies' dressing room. Six of us were in there. I caught glimpses of the other goalies as they took the net. Knowing that I was an outsider, a walk-on, I stopped sizing guys up. Nobody knew who I was anyway. Half of me didn't want to think too far ahead, the other half didn't think I had a shot. I wanted to make the team, but I never expected it. I just took the sessions one at a time. On Saturday, I didn't even know the Sunday schedule.

Over the course of the camp, the goalies started weeding themselves out. I didn't have to do anything but stop the puck. While in times past I'd worried where I fit in, this time I just worried about doing what I had to do. I was present with my task at hand. By the time Sunday even rolled around, I was still around and made it past the intra-squad game.

I was nervous and excited for that exhibition game. Regardless of the outcome, my name would be on the score sheet. I would have played a game. That in itself was an achievement. Buckling up my pads before warm-up, I felt that just playing in the game was a small win. I didn't feel the pressure to succeed because I was never supposed to be there. I was totally present in just playing that game. We ended up winning two to one and I got third star. The team asked me to register for school that Monday. I got my parents to bring me more clothes.

Over the next few weeks, my name started to appear in the paper. The starting goalie went off to his NHL camp, which was fine with me. I got more ice time and the trainer gave me one of the starter's sticks. Things were looking up, but all I kept focusing on was the next game, the next practice. I couldn't allow myself to focus on anything else. Thinking into the future would be death. I'd never get there if I didn't focus on the present. I just enjoyed coming to the rink each day because I never knew which day would be my last. I still didn't know where I fit in, so I didn't bother to figure it out. In times past, I would have thought what I could have done to manipulate my fate—a scheme. But I had what I wanted—a shot to play. I had abundance. Being in the moment allowed for this.

After exhibition, I did get sent back down, but the team had plans to bring me back. They needed to make room for me. They had to move that other goalie and a few other guys around. I just focused on developing as much as I could each game back in midget. I knew my time would come if I just focused on the process. Halfway through the year I was brought back up, and I stayed in junior for four years. Each season I got a bundle of custom sticks, extra tall with "Olynyk" stamped on them too. It all started by not thinking too far ahead at the mailbox.

Becoming Present

The paradox of winning is that to focus on the win, getting that desired outcome, you can't focus on the outcome itself. Being present with your task at hand, you're required to focus on the process. Earlier in this book, I talked about focusing on a system and letting the system do the work. Think of this as one half of the process/outcome paradox. The other half to it is being in the moment while working your system.

If you've ever watched a hockey team who goes through the motions in a game, not only will you be watching a losing team, but also you'll be watching a team that plays on its heels. The game will affect them and overtake them. As a man, you can focus on your systems and use them, even every day, but if you are not in the moment when you use them, your results will be mediocre. You'll be going through the motions, playing on your heels. The forces of the world will overtake you.

For example, one of the simplest systems to fitness is to start every day at the gym with the same warm-up routine. A routine will remove all conscious thought involved with undertaking that process and allows you to get into a state of flow. If you do not have your focus centered on your workout, it is easy to have your head elsewhere. Between worrying about work, thinking where you'll eat after and what you have to pick up on the way home, sometimes it's easy to forget about the workout itself. When you're doing sit-ups, for example, you can find yourself going to through the motions and not really feeling the tension in your core. However, with proper breathing and focus, you can feel your core tighten and crunch with each rep. Same movement, different outcome, all through the process of sitting up and down. The process must always be respected, and you respect it by living through it, giving each moment its due before worrying about the next one.

In my story above, I didn't come into training camp with the dead-set goal of making the team. My biggest goal was to have a good first ice session, then a second, then a third... Any time in my career when I thought too far ahead, whatever was ahead of me overwhelmed me. I couldn't track it because I wasn't present. It wasn't in my focus. When Portland dropped me, if I had dwelled all summer on the event and focused on the failure, surely I would be stuck in the past. The choice of where to place my focus made the difference between my career never happening and finding a new place to begin it.

This same principle of being present can even be applied to something as simple as conversations. If you've ever been to a conference you can spot the man who lacks presence immediately. The guy who is overly nice for the sake of moving the conversation forward. There is never a glitch in his speech, and all he wants to do is see if you're a good fit for his own needs and goals. Rather than enjoy the conversation (and consequently see if the business personalities are a good fit), this man forces the conversation to a fork in the road. He wants the deal too badly. It's a less effective strategy. He's thinking about where the conversation can lead rather than where it currently is. If you don't focus on the current moment, you don't know where the conversation can lead. Being present with people is key.

In any pursuit, process or purpose, the future will come regardless of what you do or do not do. It's a good thing. You can count on it. As a man, you'll see much more success in each moment if you focus on the moment itself. Do not try to force outcomes, do not try to revive the past. The future will come regardless. Take the hits as you run through the jungle of life and squeeze the juice out of every fruit while it is in your hand.

Exercise

Presence will come to you when you are open to it. The simplest way to do this is to align your mind with just one thought in the moment. The easiest thought to focus is your breath. Here is how you can focus on it to regain presence:

1. Stop whatever it is you're doing. Disengage so your mind doesn't need to focus on anything external.
2. Take a deep breath in through your nose. Use your stomach, not your chest. Put your stomach out as you inhale. Feel the air hit your nostrils.
3. Do this ten times normally.
4. Repeat the process, holding your breath for 10 seconds three times.
5. You will feel a new realignment.

This exercise not only works in day-to-day life but also between periods in hockey games.

Chapter 15
WINNERS AVOID BURNOUT

I sat on the ferry's top deck at sunset and gazed over the water. Its glow reflected one of the most beautiful parts of the world, the Sunshine Coast in British Columbia. Porpoises jumped through the water and chased the engine's rolling wake. Getting half the rain of Vancouver, the Sunshine Coast is a retired hippie's dream. It's the kind of place where you'd see a long-haired elderly lady with dangly homemade jewelry perform interpretive dances at street festivals, and where an old, bearded, draft-dodging cab driver tries to sell you a bottle of his organic blackberry wine when he drops you off. I met these people everywhere out there. I still say they share one of the most beautiful parts of Canada.

My new home on this coast would be a town called Powell River. All I knew about this place before meeting the locals was that it used to be a logging town—it had a mill at one time. Many hard-working loggers lived there still and raised families, including my wonderful billets. However, there was also a six-hour ferry-drive-ferry-drive trip from Vancouver to get there. Two ferries to urbanity. Rough logging roads carved through the mountains that could have cut this trip to an hour, but they were not drivable. The Powell River Kings were one of the most hidden junior teams in Canada. They also hadn't had a winning team in years.

I didn't choose to come to P.R; its team chose me. Two weeks earlier I had been exiled from Penticton, arguably the top program in the country. They brought me on over summer, but traded me before I could get there. Powell River picked me up. This would be my fifth junior team in four years. In hockey, a player who gets traded often is called a "suitcase," since that is what he lives out of. I took this one step further. Everything I owned could fit in the backseat of my Buick LeSabre. It was a real life Tetris—passenger seat all the way forward, pads behind the back seat, sticks through the armrest, clothes in the trunk. Luckily, that old Buick was a big car. I drove boxed-in like a New York cab driver for twenty hours over the plains and mountains of the prairies and Rockies. That's why I chose to stretch out on the top ferry deck.

When I first started making these trips at sixteen and seventeen, my parents begrudgingly supported me. They had no choice. My dad said if they didn't let me leave home to play, I probably would have run away from home in the night. I didn't argue with him on that. My entire life up to that point had revolved and expanded around hockey. It started each week as Sunday's church and ended as Saturday night's shaker. My identity was heavily tied to the sport. Everybody knew me as a hockey player. That's all they asked about. That's all I talked about. Travelling across the country to play was no big deal…the first time.

After this particular trade to P.R., I didn't feel the excitement of a new beginning. I went from a to-be dominant club, Penticton, whose goal was to win the national championship, to Powell River, who was in a rebuilding phase. I was a "twenty," a player in his final season of junior. Powell River wouldn't rebuild in one season. I also didn't have a scholarship secured yet. Schools don't give scholarships to players on rebuilding teams. As the ferry rolled back and forth hitting wave after wave, I felt very empty. I had a bad feeling about that season. I wasn't wrong.

Two and a half months later, we had three wins and fifteen losses. I would never achieve my scholarship at that pace, especially tucked away in a town that scouts couldn't reach. It was killing me and I had no way out. I wanted to quit hockey altogether.

By month three of the season, I felt despondent—feeling extreme discouragement, dejection and depression. Those three d-words were a hat trick of hopelessness. It all came to a head one night. I was finally given a game off, being the starter. We got whipped big-time by Vernon, a top team. I knew I was playing a lot (which was nice), but I hated the losing all of the time. I had been losing for three years, and those losses had worn me to the marrow. Within a matter of a month, I started hating hockey like it was a demon who had possessed me. I was losing control of my path. I had to get out, and I made a phone call I'll never forget.

"Dad, I can't do this anymore," I said, into what was then known as a payphone. The boys were eating their post-game meal in a restaurant across the street.

"What are you going to do?" he said.

"I really don't know. I just want out. I don't know."

"So, what are you going to do?"

Clearly Dad was leaving this one up to me.

"I guess I could ask for a trade," I said.

"Do what you got to do."

This one was on me.

Asking for a trade, especially in junior hockey, is a big deal. You could end up getting shipped to the end of the earth and that could be the end of your career. Fortunately for me, I was already at what seemed like the end of the earth and my career would be over in four months if I stuck around there. Asking for a trade, while daunting, seemed like it needed to be done. I couldn't stick it out any longer.

———

"What can I help you with, Olie?" said Dean. Dean was our coach. He had been recruited to come halfway across the country too after reviving a dead program in another province. I liked the guy, I really did. That's what made it so tough.

"I think we need to talk."

"Okay," he lobbed his pen on his desk and leaned back. "What's up?"

"I got made a lot of promises when I came here, and things just aren't turning out. I want a trade."

The night before I'd imagined some thunderous boom would drop from the sky through the ceiling at this moment in the conversation, like an epic climax in a black and white movie. When you ask for a trade in junior, you have little say in the matter. The manager decides an awful lot, and if you end up in the wrong spot you could get stuck there and die out. My career already felt dead. It was either go to a sixth team and try for a scholarship, or let my career die here.

"Well, a lot of us were made a lot of promises coming here," Dean said. "I'm not totally surprised. We kind of half-expected this."

Maybe.

"I just—" I said, fumbling. "I don't think I'm going to get a scholarship here and all you ever talk about is how we're rebuilding, and I'm twenty, I mean I won't be around. I'm just not loving it here. You know? It's nothing personal, just—"

"I know that," he said. "Tell me where you want to go."

I listed off my teams and leagues, all well-thought-out beforehand.

"I think we can find you a home. I'll make some calls."

That was it. It hadn't been as heavy as I'd thought. For weeks I had paced the house—one overlooking the ocean through one window and the mountains in another—and wondered if leaving was really the right move. I never thought I'd be *that* player who asks for a trade.

"You can hang out at your billet until I call you," Dean said as I left. "Don't leave town."

I hung out in Powell River for a week and got bored and then anxious. I felt twisted, sticking around the place I was ready to leave. I left town on the ferries and went to hang out with a buddy in Calgary. A week later was traded to Vernon. They were one of my dream teams to play for when I was a sixteen year-old leaving home. It rejuvenated me. I had gone from the worst team in the country to, literally, the winningest of Junior A club of all-time. The game didn't change, but my mindset did. After years of toil, I had finally landed on a bona fide winner. Winning wasn't just expected—it was the norm, the way.

In turn, I had the best playoff run of my life. We beat Penticton in the playoffs and I got my scholarship. Dean moved up to coach in the WHL, and Powell River—two years later—started a four-year run of back-to-back Coastal Championships. They became a big recruiter of top talent. Players wanted to play there. The move paid off for everybody. Winners don't stay despondent. Winners don't let themselves burn out.

Avoiding Burnout

Masculinity has a certain power and energy when it is fully harnessed. When controlled properly, it can be a force that propels a man down the tracks of his purpose like a locomotive. Many men who start chugging down this path early in their purpose, perhaps at a young age, get stuck on the rails. Adversity blocks their path. And after chasing a purpose that no longer drives them, they become weak. That locomotive force becomes a weak engine that just glides where it has to go without much force.

Now, I'm not talking about the kind of burnout here that is like a "mid-life crisis"; I'm simply not qualified to talk about that at my age. However, I do see many young men give up on their ambitions, dare I say their "dreams," because the going gets tough.

There is a key difference between giving up and pivoting though. Pivoting is a term used in the online start-up world that means changing directions when things aren't going right in a young business. You don't quit on what you're doing, but you quit what is not working for you. It's kind of like changing the forecheck or shuffling lines between periods when you're losing. You don't take off your pads and go home; you just come back with a new plan. In this chapter's story, although I really did feel like quitting hockey before my trade, I kept going. I'm glad I did this—the absolute best time of my career was ahead.

After three years of losing, I could have quit the game as a loser. I could have packed it in and hid my record from people. I could have lived with the wonder and doubt of being a loser who never knew if he could win anything. Through a little faith and sticking to it though, I got my pivot right. I landed on the best team in Canada, got a scholarship and even started my university career well until I got injured. The three years of toil put me just a step away from achievement when I asked for my trade.

For you as a man, you're going to encounter struggles. What you do with them is up to you. There are times when you need to quit doing what you're doing and find a new purpose. If you're twenty and still in Junior A, you're not going to make the NHL, but that doesn't mean you need to quit playing. There are pro opportunities, there are scholarships, and there are years of fruitful experiences to gain. Sure, you may have to change your systems or your strategies in how you play, embracing something new as you pivot toward a breakthrough year, but you can't quit when you know there is an upside within reach. This is when you pivot before burning yourself out. It's the same off the ice.

If you end up in a job you hate or a business that is floundering, or even if you go to college and chose the wrong program, know *why* you started on that path in the first place. If you feel you can still reach your goal, pivot. If you feel you have bigger goals to chase elsewhere, get out before you burn out. You will hate chasing a hopeless dead purpose and it will suck the life out of you. However, your masculine strength will be renewed with a new challenge in front of you. The younger you are, the faster your interests shift. Your life is more fluid and you have more opportunities than most men. Even if you're young, don't burn out on a dead-end purpose. Embrace a new challenge and chase it fully.

Exercise

If you feel that you are burning out on your purpose right now, use the process below. You should be able to identify your next step in rekindling the fire.

1. Ask yourself what you are truly unhappy with. Are you dissatisfied with yourself, your systems, or the path your purpose is leading you down? See where the friction lies first.
2. Ask yourself if your burnout is a result of your systems.
3. If your systems are at fault, list at least ten ways you could still chase your purpose while using a different system. This could be career-wise or outside of your job. If you find a way, change systems and keep working. This is pivoting.
4. If you find that your purpose no longer suits you, you must be open to finding a new one. Refer to Chapter One.
5. Write down your end goal of your purpose (e.g., financial freedom for your family), then the first step you need to take in achieving it with your new system.

6. Fill in the steps between the first one and the final goal. This will be your roadmap.

Chapter 16
WINNERS RESPECT MASTERY

s a Canadian kid on Saturday night, bathed and pajamaed-up before bed, you're glued to the TV, mini-stick in hand; your heroes are playing and you want to be one of them. They are the demigods of hockey. That changes. When you get a little older, slightly more schooled, you start to know why you like certain players. You don't like them as much for the color of their jersey or their awards. As you age, you become a student of the game, and you have your own games to play on Saturday nights. The players you admire and emulate are no longer arbitrary. You begin to respect the players, their talents and how they've developed their unique styles. In your learning, you discover schools of play, styles of gamesmanship, or to put it in more down-to-earth terms: you like the guys who play like you, only they play better.

Being six feet tall by the time I was thirteen, I had discovered my favorite players as well, all big goalies. Brodeur was my favorite. He handled the puck like no other and I loved that aspect of him. Obscure goalies like Roman Turek piqued my interest. Turek was a butterflying, lumbering lefty like me. He had a few good years. I also couldn't help but respect a winner like Patrick Roy who seemed to never leave his prime. One guy I liked in particular—big, aggressive, athletic—was Olaf Kolzig.

When I was a kid, Kolzig played on the Washington Capitals, as he did for a dozen-plus seasons. He had won the Vezina Trophy as the NHL's top goalie, making him top goalie in the world the year he won. That's why when I landed in Tri-City I found it a fortunate irony to have Olaf Kolzig in our dressing room.

During 2004-05, the second NHL lockout was on. This was the lockout that shifted the entire game. The whole season was cancelled, many of the game's rules changed, and all NHL players were out of work for a year. Some guys went to Europe, other guys snuck back down to the minors. Ones who had ample experience and optimism sat tight with their families. Kolzig was one of those guys.

During the lockout, he came to skate with us. In hockey, coming for a "skate" is a loose term. During a skate, a player can dog it, float around, go through the motions just to get on the ice—that floating feeling of gliding and digging in on blades, using different points of your feet than when you walk. Nothing could be more leisurely if you wanted. However, a skate can also mean coming out for a hard practice. You can't go through the motions at these. Your intensity is forced to match the other players or even go beyond them. A skate is what you make it.

Always studying, I was interested to see how Kolzig would practice. As an elite junior player you want to see what somebody better than you is doing differently, but that can leave you disappointed. The pro doesn't do anything different from the amateur. He makes the difficult look simple, the heroic look routine. He does everything you do, just better. Kolzig wasn't a finesse goaltender, but he was smart and a strong skater. The most powerful goalie I ever skated with, he could get from point A to point B as quick as the little guys who relied on speed. At six-foot-four, he didn't trip over his feet like I did, which impressed me. For me, moving in the goal crease felt like trying to dance in a telephone booth. For Kolzig, even as a big man, he made it work.

Usually, I was the first one out for practice. I liked to get a few shots in early as a pre-warm up for the warm up drills. Sometimes I'd skate laps and fire pucks at the crossbars as I passed the nets. When Kolzig joined us, I couldn't waste time like that anymore. My conscience wouldn't let me after the first time I went out with him. It astonished me at first to see him doing the most elementary of drills. Every day he started with the letters. These were simple patterns every goalie learns when he first straps on the pads. They are the scales of the goaltender's piano. Out and back to the post, then across the goal line, then out again, Kolzig crossed out the X. Push after push, he formed the W, then the Y, then he'd do it over again doing butterflies at each stop. There was nothing fancy about these drills. I'd done them a million times before. What I admired was that an NHLer, a top one, would start off his day in practice by doing basic drills. But it made sense—everything great in his game started from strong skating, from those very basic movements.

When fans watch a game and see a goalie make a huge save, it is often because that goalie is out of position. He needs to stretch and dive for what looks miraculous. However, the best goalies just let the puck hit them in the chest. While I flailed and dived, Kolzig took it square every time. His minimalist moves were a direct result of his positioning, and he was always positioned like a master due to his strong skating. That mastery started with perfecting the basics, each day. It's doing less, not more, and that's mastery of the fundamentals.

Respecting Mastery

The title of this chapter is not about one man respecting another who is a master of a trade. Mastery itself is the noun in this case, like a virtue. There has been a rapid loss of respect for trades, crafts and well-honed abilities today amongst men. We live in a tremendous society, but we also jump from one pursuit to the next without giving these pursuits the effort they deserve to get good at them. We do jobs, but we aren't dedicated to crafts. The man who expects to just pick up a guitar, dive into day trading, or dangle his way through an entire team before learning the fundamentals has lost already. If he hasn't put in the requisite effort, i.e., failures, to know the pursuit inside and out he is only kidding himself. He has to be in it for the long haul.

How disrespectful it is to the art of playing the guitar if a man picks one up, learns a few chords, takes a few lessons and then quits because he says he doesn't have time. If he laments that he doesn't have the time to practice, then why would he even begin? If a man sets a purpose that he wants to master the guitar to the point that he can be a performing musician—different than a hobby—he has to accept that working his fingers raw learning the basic chords are what lay his foundation to greatness. Just as Keith Richards made his claim off of mastering those simple chords, the prodigy needs to learn how these chords simply work. Before he can begin the advanced solos that have that sexy effect on your ear, he needs that foundation. In the end, the odds of he becoming the next Keith Richards are largely against him, but to be a master of the guitar, to be in that top one per cent, is definitely achievable—just think of the millions of guitars collecting dust in closets and corners out there. If the player respects the process of learning the dull habits, the sexy stuff will come.

Mastery is knowing your craft so well that you can pinpoint the cause and effect actions that create your results. You know the miniscule details and why they matter where others do not even see them. You know all the rules surrounding the trade so well that you also know when to break them for an even better effect. You have complete unconscious competence in what you do so all you need to worry about is being present with the task.

In this chapter's story, I talk of Olaf Kolzig doing skating drills. What impressed me the most about watching Kolzig was nothing flashy. What I really respected was how he would start and stop in net. Rather than use the whole blade of his skate to push off and stop when moving around the crease, he would push off and stop using just the toe of his blade. He told us that it created a greater power and control when moving. I instantly implemented his advice, and that three-inch shift in my foot created an increase in the speed of my movements. Furthermore, once I realized he was doing this, I could see that he not only pushed and stopped off of his toe, but also that he did it every time. He could be alone doing the most elementary drills before practice or literally be in the Stanley Cup finals. It was always that same push.

At the same time, the wisdom of years of mastery came into play. An overlooked fact of pro hockey players is that they are really the only ones on earth who continue the game in earnest after age twenty-two. Many men play recreationally after that age, but pros can play almost twice as long as the typical competitive player. Their mastery is incredibly deep. The reason they can make a save or goal look effortless is because they've been putting in twice as much concentrated effort as the typical elite player. How many people are willing or able to do this in their pursuits?

After evolving this effort for years, over and over, the man with mastery sees simple things and develops simple truths that ring much deeper. For instance, Kolzig alerted me to the fact that as a big goalie, I faced fewer shots than smaller guys. By taking up more of the net and cutting down more of the angle, I forced the shooter to shoot wider in order to not hit me. And, when he shot too wide, he missed the net.

"When a shooter misses the net because of your size, it's as good as a save. Small guys have to work harder," he said. Having that perception alone can put one's mind at ease, but it only comes from years of being in the trenches.

Mastery is as much about the tangible skills required to be a master of the craft as it about the master's mindset. The master's mindset is a winner's mindset. To develop a master's mindset, you must respect the process of giving applied, consistent effort to your craft. The years of playing hockey or mastering any purpose must be done through full immersion. You can't become a master by being a weekend warrior. In the entrepreneurial world, without fail, I don't think I've ever heard an expert or successful businessman say he doesn't devour books. Reading about other masters and studying other masters not only provides inspiration that can further your applied, consistent effort, but it also gives knowledge and spawns new ideas. This can come in many ways. For me, doing the skating drills before every practice was immersion. Attending marketing conferences and coming home with a handful of new ideas to test is immersion. Reading a book and adopting a new idea is immersion. Immersion keeps the mental doors of applied, consistent effort open.

Once you attain a level of mastery in your craft, you should never lose the fundamental ability to apply the skill or to consult on it for others. You will have such a tight grasp of the never-changing fundamentals that you will be able to navigate any situation that could come to you. Give a man a fish, he eats for a day. Teach a man to fish, he eats for a lifetime. Master the art of fishing, and you can teach the whole damn village to be your fleet of fishermen.

By adopting a mastery mindset and staying the course through the highs and lows, even expecting them, you can build skills and earn a mindset that few men experience. Once that is in place, it can never be taken away from you. It will also be the reference experience etched into your mind that will enable you to take on other pursuits with the expectation of success. Nothing is nobler than mastering your purpose.

Finally, you must realize that you will never be perfect and never be complete at your purpose. Pushing forward opens more doors for you, and as you learn more you'll start seeing that new avenues of exploration appear. You'll separate yourself from others. Your vision will become more acute and possibilities will reveal themselves through all of the action you've taken. Mastery is a destiny, not a destination. The honing of skills never ends.

Exercise

There is no magic formula to becoming a master of your purpose. You must live it every day, you must have a clear vision of what you seek in mind. You must meditate on it constantly. It should be a hunger and a destiny for you.

In shaping this destiny, resolve to say the following to yourself everyday:

"I will do whatever it takes to master [this skill]. There is no try. I have all the time in the world to reach the highest level possible, as soon as possible. This is what I do now."

Make a resolution that there is no turning back on mastering your purpose. That is why you're here.

Chapter 17

WINNERS UNDERSTAND HOW TO LOSE

Shaking hands at center ice could have felt like humiliation. Our team, the Vernon Vipers, had broken down two minutes earlier. Trapped in our own end, the puck pinned between our winger's skates and the boards, one of the Nanaimo Clippers' forwards fed it back to their point man. His comrades bolted for the front of the net to screen me.

I was experienced at twenty years old. I'd seen this play hundreds of times before. I was big enough to see over the crafty little buggers in front of me.

As the shot came from the blue line, not all that hard, I moved into it. I made the gentle drop onto a knee, jamming my pads together to close the five-hole. I even lowered my glove to get my hand on the shot. No rebound to result. After weeks on the road and games every second night, this was about as routine as it would get. That's when the shot got tipped.

What should have been a simple save was a deflection over my glove. The puck should have landed in my hand a foot off the ice, but it hit the blade of a stick and careened a few inches higher. I wasn't outstretched, I wasn't too late. I was just human. A photographer caught the shot perfectly. I still have it.

Nanaimo jumped and cheered. They had won the league championship. All thirty-five hundred of our fans were quiet. Our boys hunched over and stared at the ice. I lumbered up to my feet. It was as clean of a dirty deflection one could make. Weeks of proudly playing with separated ribs and partially torn groins all gave way to pain for our guys. Heavy hearts beat a little slower.

Lining up to shake hands, I couldn't feel bad. Nobody could be blamed. We really couldn't do much more. I knew the only difference between us and them was fourth line depth and a deflection. They had one more talented line, so they could play their system a little tighter. They had one more play that made a deflection work. When you get down to the league finals, almost two months deep in playoffs, you can see the truth. After repeatedly playing teams over and over, and after seeing your guys perform night in, night out, reality is obvious. You don't work on plays and mistakes by that point—you won't make it to that point if that's what you're working on. You're just honing the system, keeping your mind in shape. The rehearsal is over; it's time to dance.

And when that dance ended, we left empty handed. Whenever a team loses out of playoffs you see the old guys bury their heads and cry. Tears stream down their face like children. Some will never again play the game they've played their whole life. Others move on to higher levels, but the fun and battle and majesty that came with playing junior ends. I just felt empty. No tears, no reflection. That was that, junior was done for me. Six teams in four years and finally I was on one that could win something. I was happy not to be a loser; I was proud to go out on top, despite the final loss.

When I shook hands before exiting the ice I congratulated the other team. They were every dirty name in the book, but they were good. Four years of my preparation and practice went into reaching that league final. The work paid off. The next week, I chose my scholarship from five offers. I had made it as far as I could with the skills I had. I had proven to myself that I wasn't some perennial backup loser. I could win—I just needed to learn how. Once you learn those lessons you don't forget them. The lessons, the memories and the hockey are always with you.

Shaking the final hand in line, I pivoted right and exited through the players' bench. Thirty-five hundred people were still on their feet, the gracious applauders, the supporters. I took one last look around the rink, knowing that I would never be in that position again. That was as far as I would get. My crowning glory was being a backup to truly sensational top-tier guys and being an all-star at the second tier when it was too late.

Through it all, I learned a load of lessons. I had been ripped on by coaches, congratulated by teammates, and travelled regions of the world most kids in my hometown never saw. I had grown into something bigger doing something I loved.

Learning to Lose

Throughout my career, my goalie coaches always told me I was too hard on myself. We'd get outshot forty to twenty and lose two to one, and I'd shoulder the blame for not carrying us further. Losing is frustrating. Everybody hates it, and in junior hockey you're consciously conditioned to hate it.

You have to take a step back, though. Losing should not be taken lightly, but it should also be taken for what it is. Sometimes a loss is from a lack of effort, or a lack of focus or something within your control that you ignored. However, losing, especially in a team scenario, can be out of your control.

Overachievers seek to control their losses. They aren't supposed to lose. They are bred winners. While my favorite players and parents to advise are winners, often what I'm doing is helping them to handle losses. Overachievers get focused on outcomes because they are results driven. This can be good. It can be motivating. You need some carrot at the end of the stick. At the same time, winners can never lose sight of the process and all the incremental gains they make throughout it.

I'm going to assume you're an overachiever, falling into the winner's category or sliding into it—otherwise you wouldn't read a book like this. That means you're probably susceptible to being hard on yourself. You may become so focused on your goals that you can forget the process on the way to them. It happens more often than you'd think.

The overachiever needs to take a Zen approach to his learning and purpose. Every day, you must focus on the process and move the mountain that is your purpose one stone at a time. Some days, the rocks will come tumbling down on you. You can't let that stop you from picking one up the next day. When your purpose is to move the mountain, your process is to move the rocks one at a time. Whether you move today's rock successfully or not doesn't matter tomorrow. You have to arrive and pick up your rock everyday. That's process.

In my story above, finally getting the chance to be a bona fide winner, I (and our team) lost right at the wire. It wasn't from a lack of effort. We showed up every day and ran the process as close to perfection as we could. Most days we even ramped up our effort more than the previous day. And in the end, we still lost. Our purpose was to finish as champions. We came out as runner-ups. Nobody remembers the wedding by who was the bridesmaid.

But, that said, I achieved something very important in that process. After years of being a perennial loser on the score sheet, I got a real taste of what winning felt like. Not only did I get the high fives around town and my name in the paper—all of the superfluous stuff that doesn't really matter—but I also felt my greatest sense of purpose and duty. Every day at the rink, I was relied upon. I knew that I needed to show up. I had core purpose to others. If I didn't play well, we didn't win. That's the life of a starting goalie. Ultimately, we did lose. It stung. It hurt. Yet, I knew that I had the *capability* to win. It allowed me to hold my head high.

If you look at the greatest men in history, the political leaders, the entrepreneurs, the philanthropists and even the athletes, every one goes through some kind of struggle at some point. History is littered with examples. Crazy Horse was stripped of his war leader's shirt before becoming the most legendary native warrior ever. Nelson Mandela spent twenty-seven years in prison before transforming a nation and the world. Steve Jobs built a revolutionary company, lost it, and brought it back to be the highest valued company ever. These struggles built strength. These losses hold great lessons not only for the men who endured them, but also for others who have looked up to them.

Knowing that when you lose, you don't always have control, that you are always one man, and most importantly that you will get back on the process to achieving your purpose the next day, will allow you to be a winner in the long run. The unshakable belief in yourself through small victories and through tough losses can build real character. The *masculine* thrives and grows from challenge. It require action to grow. There may be no greater challenge than bouncing back from a loss.

Following the loss I wrote about in this chapter's story, I received a handful of offers to come play for universities throughout Canada. Me, the guy who sat on the bench more than he played, the guy who really only had half of a winning season. The fact was that I also learned how to win, I aligned with the right people, and I figured out a process that carried me through. It took me four years, but I did it. Now I work to pass those lessons along to young players and young men alike. Getting up to write this book every morning has been part of my new process.

When you've faced adversity, through loss and doubt, you can draw on it to create courage. Keep your belief that your purpose is your destiny. Just as I heard before my first junior game, "Play the system, and let the system do the work," you need to keep going through the process—your system—and providence will shift one way or another. Winners can't be held down once they figure out their *own* process to win. They'll pivot and shift and morph, as will their purpose, until an alignment is reached. There is really no exercise for this.

The task falls to you to trust in yourself, your purpose and your systems. Cherish your wins, rebound from your losses, and show up the next day ready to do it again. This is the winner's way.

Chapter 18
WINNERS CONTRIBUTE

Have you ever met a junior hockey player who has been drafted, dropped, listed, offered NCAA and pro opportunities, played Canadian university, lived in twelve billet households, been traded, called up, sent down, changed high schools five times in one year, gotten pestered by agents, appeared on national TV, seen teammates get thrown in the drunk tank with their pants around their ankles, asked for a trade, had mid-season surgery, been on loan as an all-star and been on the bench watching future NHL all-stars…all while playing every level from ages fourteen to twenty-one?

That player was me, and that's the bio on my website, Junior Hockey Truth.com. Junior hockey taught me more about the "real world" than any formal education ever could. The lessons in this book are only a sliver of my experience. Most players don't get cut and swapped as much as I did, and through my ice-guided travels I learned more about junior hockey than most players do in a lifetime.

When I was nineteen, I started a blog to keep my friends back home updated just on what I was doing. Every season, I'd travel half the country. While they were all in university, or on the oil rigs or travelling, I was playing hockey. That was my life, and I loved it. As I finished junior, I was writing weird essays and short stories in conjunction with a literature class I took at the local community college. For a guy who cared enough about high school to merit a 'D' in high school English, I was awestruck to receive back an essay from my professor with a short note. "A+. You have a talent. Explore this." Not being an idiot felt good. I took his advice.

Once removed from junior hockey, I started to see it differently. As you age, you don't think back in a video stream. You just see stills and your mind creates captions for them. You rewrite a bit of your own history between the stills but the main points never go away. Every time I thought back to my playing days, I kept thinking about how little the media, fans and outsiders knew about what actually happened on a junior team. The season before, our captain played with bruised ribs all through playoffs, his centerman also couldn't lift his hand above his shoulder, and our bus broke down on the road the night before and we couldn't sleep. We lost the next day and got chastised for it. I knew the world only cared about results. However, I also realized that a lot of the world didn't know what went on beneath the stands. Painting that view would illuminate what goes on in junior hockey. I could write a book.

Of course, it would be foolish to do this at twenty-one. How could I write a book at that age? Who would take me seriously? Looking back, questions like these are the reason I coach young men today. Why should age matter? If you produce results, who cares? Five years later at twenty-six, I daydreamed away from my work one afternoon, wrote a list of every facet of junior hockey that came to me and started writing my first book for two hours per day every day (My system, wink wink.) Nervous, I launched it online, told myself it didn't matter how it did, and watched it do well. Then it started to matter.

I saw the need to help young players, usually ages thirteen to seventeen, make it to junior hockey. Then their parents started emailing, and calling and requesting more info. The Junior Hockey Truth website was born.

Today I travel North America giving speeches to young players and their parents. My mission is to help them succeed at the dream of playing junior hockey. Between my books, products and website, I not only educate parents about their sons' options, but I also do coaching with their sons to help get them to the next level. There are novels worth of info waiting to be written for hockey players about their mental game. I want to use that info to help not only hockey players, but young men everywhere. The need is alive.

Daily, I receive emails from parents thanking me for putting up new videos, or asking me questions about my *Training Camp Invite Formula*. I get to give back in the same way that I wished somebody would have given back to me when I was a kid struggling to make junior.

The Junior Hockey Truth allows me to contribute and give back in a way that is wholeheartedly fulfilling. My biggest challenge is often delegating away work I don't need to do because I love the minutiae. Editing interviews with coaches is fun when you like hearing the interview over and over. It takes me back to a time when I was that hopeful player. That time won't come back to me, and I made peace with that a long time ago. Now my mission is to help others, and that is a huge win that has come from my career.

Every man should find some time and some way to help give back to his community. You don't necessarily have to build libraries across the country or try to solve the biggest health problem in Africa to feel like you've given back. Gratitude is powerful, and knowing what you're grateful for can often be a first step to helping. I am grateful for my hockey career. It forced me to leave home earlier than I would have, putting me in uncomfortable and trying situations that I never would have entered on my own accord. I was challenged and confronted many times by coaches and teammates to be accountable and contribute. In short, I learned to develop the courage and consistency to win through many battles. Most young men are not so privileged—yes, privileged—to get their minds mentally strapped by the leather of playing high level junior hockey. By helping others, I hope to give them that same opportunity and head start. It's too deep in me to forget what hockey did for me.

Contributing

Giving back or "contributing" is beyond valuable to the psyche of a man and the health of his community. On the surface, we know this stuff to be good—it's what good people do, that kind of thing. Few stop to look at how that contribution enlivens the masculine spirit.

Contributing helps you win in multiple ways. You're providing irrefutable evidence to the world that you have something to offer. You are a person of value. You matter to somebody. It's serving unselfishly because you can. And no matter how much bravado puffs from your chest as you enter a room, you likely needed a contribution from somebody—a parent, a teacher, a coach—to get there. Your mind cannot doubt your importance to the world when it knows that people need what you can offer. The mind knows you have value. You matter.

I remember one time playing with a fighter who had tremendous fisticuff upside but weak skills. He worked harder than anybody else after practice, trying to force improvement on his critical weaknesses. Yet, during every second period, the one where I'd open the forwards' door, he'd shuffle right up to the door and go, "Watch Olie. I'll be right back down." Sure enough, the coach would call out another line and our fighter would go right back down the bench. That season, there were five games when he didn't play a single shift but just sat on the bench (Definitely a case where you bond with the backup.) The more I thought about it, the fighter truly doesn't want to play the pity shift. He doesn't want that one shift with two minutes left just so he can touch the ice after sitting on the bus for five hours. He just wants to fulfill his purpose. That fighter just wants his thirty seconds of glory because that is what makes him important to the team. Our fighter couldn't skate, couldn't hit the net at all with his shot, but he could swing. His value was in his fists and face. When he could fight he was *our* maverick and he was glowing from the pride of it. Sometimes that meant giving up his face to contribute.

When you feel you have little to give, when you feel down on your purpose in life, when you're trying to go further and reach a new level, the most important thing you can do is give. The only way to receive a pass is to give the puck to somebody else. You're more likely to have the puck find you when you give it away.

Contributing is also important because it draws people toward you. There is no greater sign of having value than giving it away. Everybody wants to support the guy who is helping them. It's not just the actual act of giving that becomes a signpost of your value, but also that you're opening the channels of reciprocity. It's in human nature that we feel the need for reciprocity. When we receive something we have a built in obligation mechanism to give back. It's how we would maintain our tribal societies, and it's also how successful teams function.

When you are clear on your purpose in life and you are willing to give more than you receive, the contribution will come back to you in one form or another. People want to be around people who give because everybody wants to be around people of value. They want to be around winners. On the ice, everybody who wants to be a goal scorer desires to play with the setup man with soft hands. At the party after, it doesn't matter who scored, everybody wants to be around the guy who can talk to the girls. Every guy wants a good wingman in life's battles.

Of course, another great reason for contribution is that it feels good. Helping feels good; it's wired in us so we do it more. We are selfish creatures by nature, but we are giving by heart because selfishness only takes us so far. Being wired to reciprocate, we feel the need to give. Like most things in life, it's a result of an age old survival mechanism.

When you contribute you build confidence in knowing you have something to offer. You will pull others toward your purpose and feel good in the process. It's really one of the best things a man can do to progress as he is progressing on his purpose. Whenever you want the golden pass, give one first.

Exercise

Like I said, contribution doesn't have to be major to be effective. It also doesn't have to be at a soup kitchen or a charity. There are many ways to give. Here's how to find your way:

1. Get your own life together first. You can't contribute until you have the ability to take care of yourself.
2. Pick something you enjoy doing or something that you are good at, or both. It could also be an area you have great knowledge in.
3. Find an organization or group that is dedicated to your knowledge area. For instance, if you are particularly fond of math, find a website that pairs tutors with students.
4. Make a commitment. Set aside time each week focus on this activity. As little as one hour per week is ample. If you feel you are too busy, be adamant. The time you set aside to give away will force you to be more productive. It will create more time for you in the long run.

Afterword
JUNIOR HOCKEY TRUTH

renner and Mitch sat to my left holding each other and sobbing; Jacs buried his head in his hands to my right. I didn't know what to do. If there was a definition for the "agony of defeat," I was seeing it on both sides of me. These guys were twenty year-olds and it was their last game of junior. Their last game forever.

All four of us were pulled from different parts of the country—a mix of farm boys, heirs of business empires and princes of hockey lineage. We'd never play together again, and within a few years, we wouldn't be playing hockey again. Brenner had already had his NHL tryout. He was destined to play for pay. Mitch was off to some obscure college to find a wife and a piece of paper. Jacs and I had decided to go to university and keep playing. We both lasted a year doing that. Yet, beyond the vale of tears, we were the most grateful guys in that room—we had the chance to play hockey non-stop for four years, every day. It got us free school, a little bit of money to spend while we were there, and the chance to live the dream for just a little bit.

"This will be the greatest time of your life, men," Mitch had said a couple months early at the start of playoffs. He was right.

Before I played junior hockey, I didn't really know what to expect. Sure, I had the Internet and I could look at the schedules and had visited the rinks, but I didn't know the real story. So many people had told me, "Get your school, get your school" like university was the Holy Grail to life. It seemed *too* obvious.

Others said, "You only get one shot. Go pro if you can." One guy retorted to this, "Go pro if you want to end up on your ass at twenty-five in some town in South Carolina, washing cars at some used car dealership your girlfriend's dad owns." That made me think.

I had all of these options ahead of me, and I was only fifteen years old. I only wanted to go to school because that was what I was told I was supposed to do. So really, I didn't care if I *wanted* school. I was just told that is what you do, so I knew to shoot for it. Truthfully, I didn't know the right answer for me.

One year, a tier I major junior team would tell me that they played in the best league in the world and would cover my education, which was true. However, the next year, a tier II junior A league would say that they got the most American scholarships and would give me more time to develop long-term. That was true too. It was a lot of decision making for a fifteen year-old because I had to align with a side.

At the age of fifteen, young players in Canada and the United States have to decide where they want to go with their hockey careers. The colleges recruit players from one set of junior leagues, and the pros recruit from another. Beneath these sets of junior leagues are a feedlot full of fifteen year-olds who begin to align their future with one set. The hitch is that regardless of which set you choose, both can lead to the NHL. So it becomes a contest of what kind of free school can you get while you're there and which route gives you the best shot at the Show. It's kind of like a regular kid choosing where to take his Masters or Ph.D. but at fifteen before he has a bachelors degree. You don't know the future, and you decide it before you leave the 'GO' square on the board.

I ended up bouncing between both sets of leagues. I got three years of Canadian school paid for in full, and a little extra money for the fourth year. I received an English degree by handing in the appropriate length of essays on time with minimal effort—I focused on starting a business while not in class. I took school over pro and probably have more to show for it, on paper and in life experience outside of hockey. I got lucky. I learned enough from junior hockey to write a whole book of lessons. I realized this only a year or two after I was done junior. That's why I created the Junior Hockey Truth.

JHT is a book and website for parents and players in bantam and midget hockey, ages thirteen to seventeen. My mission is to help these players reach junior and succeed when they get there. So far, the response has been overwhelming. Every league puts out tons of information about why they are the best, but nobody had been disseminating it, and nobody talks about the day-to-day of being a junior player.

There are thousands of bantam and midget hockey players in North America looking into the future, wondering what it would be like to play junior hockey in their country. More importantly, these players often want to know the most efficient ways to get there. In an athletic life that is too short to learn by trial and error, these players want to get it right the first time. They want to play their seasons and actually get noticed for tryouts. They want to go to their tryouts and actually make an impact. They want to talk to that junior coach and be ready for the questions he's going to ask them. I thought it was unfortunate to play for six teams in my four-year junior career. It turned out that my suitcase-style would be a major benefit in learning how junior hockey works, and now I can bring that from behind the scenes to center ice.

If you're a parent who is committed to your son's future, or if you're a player who wants to play junior hockey, I encourage you to check out my online community at www.juniorhockeytruth.com. There you will find articles, tips, message boards, and my other books and products where you can learn what it takes to make it at junior hockey. If you're ready to take the next step toward junior, download my free videos at www.juniorhockeybook.com. It's all there for you to explore and educate yourself the easy way.

And when you do take that first step, I look forward to seeing you online and wish you the best of luck in your career.

ACKNOWLEDGEMENTS

I must give a few thank you notes here…

First, I'd like to thank all the guys who appeared in here, real names, composites or otherwise. Without you, there would be no book. Secondly, I'd like to thank all of my coaches and teammates over the years who taught me something. The foundation for my life's success was built in dressing rooms around the continent and you guys were those rooms with me. Without a doubt, I must also thank my friend Jesse Krieger, author of Lifestyle Entrepreneur. Jesse introduced me to our publisher Morgan James and has been on my Junior Hockey Truth journey since day one. Buy his book today!

Lastly, I have to thank my family—parents, Ivan and Phyllis; sister, Roxanne; my grandparents, aunts and uncles, neighbors, and all the rest of you who supported me throughout my career and continue to do so today. Simply thank you.

Oh yes... I can't forget to tip my glass to Colin Dudeck and Bryan Kolodziejski. You're always been the ones who've helped me avoid burnout.

ABOUT THE AUTHOR

 Have you ever met a junior hockey player who has been drafted, dropped, listed (on teams in three provinces and one state), been offered NCAA and pro opportunities, played as a CIS player, lived in 12 billet households, been traded, called up, sent down, changed high schools five times in one year, pestered by agents, appeared on national TV, seen teammates get thrown in the drunk tank with their pants around their ankles, asked for a trade, had mid-season surgery, been on loan as an all-star and been on the bench watching future NHL all-stars…all while playing every level from ages 14 - 21?

Nick Olynyk is that player. He is also called "North America's junior hockey expert" and has written numerous books for bantam and midget hockey parents and players. His website is www.juniorhockeytruth.com. Check it out today.

CPSIA information can be obtained
at www.ICGtesting.com
Printed in the USA
LVOW12s1642280817
546678LV00003B/720/P